A SOCIAL HISTORY OF ARCHAEOLOGY:
THE BRITISH EXPERIENCE

A Social History of Archaeology

THE BRITISH EXPERIENCE

Kenneth Hudson

The humanistic science which we call by the clumsy name of archaeology.
Sir Mortimer Wheeler,
1948, in a BBC radio programme

First published 1981 by
THE MACMILLAN PRESS LTD
London and Basingstoke
Companies and representatives
throughout the world

ISBN 0 333 25679 4

Filmset by Vantage Photosetting Co. Ltd,
Southampton and London

Printed in Hong Kong

Contents

List of Illustrations

1. Professor Martin Biddle.
2. Robert Munro, F.S.A.
3. Mill Stephenson, F.S.A.
4. The Right Rev. G. F. Browne.
5–7. Three meetings of the Somersetshire Archaeological and Natural History Society.
8. General Pitt-Rivers.
9. Excavations at Cranborne Chase.
10, 11. Two members of General Pitt-Rivers' staff in the 1880s and 1890s.
12. Artist's impression (1911) of life in Meare Lake Village, Somerset.
13–15. Excavation and re-erection at Stonehenge, 1901–2.
16. Excavation at the Sanctuary, Wiltshire, June 1930.
17. Roman pavement unearthed in London, 1869.
18, 19. The *Illustrated London News* sends its artist to Mycenae.
20. Sir Leonard Woolley and his foreman Hamoudi.
21. Dramatising Woolley's discoveries at Ur, 1923.
22. Sir Flinders Petrie on site at Memphis.
23. Sir Max Mallowan.
24. Lord Carnarvon and Howard Carter at the tomb of Tutankhamun.
25. Gold tomb figure.
26. Alabaster vase.
27. Figurine.
28. Sir Arthur Evans at Knossos.
29. Dr Mortimer Wheeler's methods at Maiden Castle in the 1930s.
30. Dr Wheeler displayed his Maiden Castle graves with brilliant showmanship.
31. Watching the natives at work.
32. Maiden Castle, 1934. Dr Wheeler's tourist altars.
33, 34. Two of the famous Maiden Castle postcards.
35. Piltdown Man, 1913.
36. Artist's reconstruction of Viroconium, 1925.
37. Sir Mortimer Wheeler and Dr Glyn Daniel testing the Iron Age gruel.
38. Sir Mortimer Wheeler talks to Magnus Magnusson in the first of two *Chronicle* films.

Acknowledgements

Among the many people and institutions who have helped me to gather material for this book and who have given me the benefit of their advice in shaping my ideas, I should like to mention especially the following:
F. K. Annable, of the Museum of the Wiltshire Archaeological and Natural History Society; Frank Atkinson; Neil Cossons; Beatrice de Cardi; Desmond Hawkins; Roy Hayward; Museum of London; R. N. R. Peers, of the Dorset County Museum; Jennifer Price of Salisbury and South Wiltshire Museum; Dr C. A. Ralegh Radford; Michael Rix; The Société Guernsiaise; The Somerset Archaeological and Natural History Society; Ray Sutcliffe; Nicholas Thomas, of Bristol City Museums; and F. V. Thompson, of the Society of Antiquaries.

The author and publishers would like to thank the following who have kindly given permission for the use of copyright material: Winchester

Excavations Committee (1); the Society of Antiquaries (2, 3); Surrey Archaeological Society (4); Somerset Archaeological Society (5–7); Salisbury and South Wiltshire Museum(8–11); the *Illustrated London News* (12, 17, 18–19, 21, 35 and 36); Devizes Museum (13–15, 16 and 47); Shaftesbury Museum (20); Department of Egyptology, University College, London (22); Camera Press Ltd (23); the Griffith Institute, Ashmolean Museum, Oxford (24–8); Dorset County Museum (29–34, 40 and 41); the BBC (37–9); the Museum of London (42–5); W. F. Tipping (46); Portsmouth City Museum (48); Ann Nicholls (49, 53–4); A. J. Percival (50); the Borough of Thamesdown (51–2); and Frank Hawtin (55).

Introduction

'Much,' observes Glyn Daniel, 'has been written on the history of British archaeology'[1] and this is most certainly true. It is curious, therefore, that so little attempt has been made to relate the practice of archaeology to the social conditions of the time, to see how money, the educational and political system and the class structure have determined both the selection and ambitions of archaeologists and the way in which they have set about their work. The present book tries to fill this gap. It looks at the kind of people who have been influential in archaeology from mid-Victorian times onwards, at the methods by which archaeological work has been financed, at the prestige which has been given to archaeologists and their achievements, and at the extent to which they have felt obliged to explain themselves and their activities to the general public.

Inevitably, there will be considerable discussion of personalities. No subject develops without people or in a social vacuum, and one can notice, with hindsight, certain key figures who have been instrumental in changing archaeology's direction, men and in one or two instances women blessed with unusual energy and imagination, who have felt the need for a new approach and who have been sensitive to changes in the political and philosophical climate. They are not always the obvious people and, when one regards archaeology from the point of view of society, rather than of the professional or the academic world, some re-assessment of reputations is inevitable. Such a change of emphasis will, for example, bring Tessa Wheeler out of the shadows unintentionally cast by her much better known husband.

This is a book about archaeology as it has been carried out by the British and against the background of British life, prejudices and opportunities. But British archaeology, like the British way of life, has done very well abroad and it makes little sense to think of it in insular terms. For several generations, the governing class of these islands was accustomed to working abroad and it had the political skills needed to do this satisfactorily and, in some cases, brilliantly. Helped and encouraged by the Army and Navy and by the Imperial tradition, it had immense confidence in its dealings with foreigners of all races and, since, with remarkably few exceptions, British archaeologists until at least the 1930s were members of the British governing class, they usually displayed the attitudes and values of that class, whether they happened to be working at home or overseas.

What British archaeologists achieved overseas, indeed, was largely responsible for narrowing the meaning of the word 'archaeology'. In Crete, in Egypt, in Mesopotamia and elsewhere in the Middle East and around the Mediterranean, the great discoveries which caught the attention of the public were made as the result of digging. Sir Leonard Woolley, Sir Arthur Evans, Sir Max Mallowan and others earned their knighthoods and made their reputations by their skill and good fortune in finding wonderful things underneath vast quantities of sand and earth. They were the excavator-knights, the finders of buried treasure, who fired the imagination of their fellow countrymen and brought archaeology to the attention of the popular press and therefore of the man in the street. Since the 1920s, archaeology, for most people, has been practically a synonym for excavation.

Any social history of British archaeology must begin with an examination of what 'archaeology' and 'archaeologist' mean and have meant to British people, since the language is common property. This is not to disregard the fact that some people use words with more precision and sensitivity than others, or that educated people have a special responsibility to express themselves carefully, to take full advantage of the possibilities of the language. As a former Master of the Rolls, Lord Denning has put it, with the duties of his own profession particularly in mind: 'We are not the slaves of words, but their masters. We sit here to give them their natural and ordinary meaning in the context in which we find them.'[2]

That is all anyone can do, within the legal world or outside it. We may regret new expressions or changes in the meaning of old ones, but we have neither the power nor the right to deny they have happened. We can do no more than record the facts and assess their significance, and the facts relating to 'archaeology' are that between about 1910 and 1930 it narrowed its meaning and during the 1960s and 1970s it has shown signs of dissatisfaction with that narrowness.

During the Victorian and Edwardian periods, 'archaeology' was used in a very general sense. As an illustration of this, one might instance a paper, 'The Archaeology of the West Cumberland Coal Trade', written by Isaac Fletcher and published in the *Transactions of the Cumberland and Westmorland Antiquarian and Archaeological Society* – the title is significant – in 1878. Fletcher was an astronomer and Fellow of the Royal Society, that is, a person with an established reputation as a scientist. To make a careful study of the Cumberland coal industry was a hobby activity for him, the kind of thing that any civilised man, no matter what his profession, might reasonably want to do. To him 'archaeology' meant no more or less than the study of the past which was based on the observation of its tangible remains. In his paper he therefore referred as easily and naturally to 'the archaeology of the steam

1. *Professor Martin Biddle on location in Winchester, 1965.*

engine' as to 'the archaeology of the coal trade'. Then as now, 'the history of the steam engine' or 'the history of the coal trade' would not have expressed the same meaning or reflected the same approach. 'Archaeology' was the proper word to describe the investigations of a man who considered it important to collect much of his evidence in the field, instead of confining himself to what he could find in a library. So Isaac Fletcher worked through pay bills and other day-to-day papers, visited mines and talked to old miners. So far as we know, he never called himself an archaeologist, let alone an industrial archaeologist, but there is not the slightest doubt that he regarded what he was doing as archaeology. The fact that he had excavated nothing would have seemed completely irrelevant.

What significance, if any, are we to see in his Society's name, 'the Cumberland and Westmorland Antiquarian and Archaeological Society'? At that time, the two words 'antiquarian' and 'archaeological' were used very loosely, but, to most people, the first probably referred to a broad interest in the past and the second more specifically to an interest in historic objects, evidence which one could see and touch. It is worth continuing this exercise a little further, in view of later and often heated disagreements as to what archaeology really consisted of and what archaeologists should and should not be doing.

The *Oxford English Dictionary* is very useful in this connection, not least because its definitions are now at least half a century out of date. The volume which deals with the letter A was published in 1933 and we can safely assume that the primary work on its was finished two or three years before that date, if not earlier. This contains, of course, the entries for 'antiquary', 'antiquity', 'archaeology' and 'archaeologist'. They are as follows:

> '*Antiquary* A student (usually a professed student) or collector of antiquities. Formerly used, in a wide sense, of a student of early history; now tending to be restricted to one who investigates the relics and monuments of the more recent past.'
> '*Antiquity* (now usually pl.; formerly sing. or collect.) Remains or monuments of antiquity; ancient relics.'
> '*Archaeology* 1. Ancient history generally; systematic description or study of antiquities.
> 2. The scientific study of the remains and monuments of the prehistoric period.'
> '*Archaeologist* A professed student of archaeology.'

The examples given as illustrations of usage indicate that, in the view of the editors, attention has to be paid in establishing a definition, to the development of professionalism among students of the past. A quotation given under *archaeologist* and dated 1880 says: 'The archaeologists have raised the study of antiquities to the rank of a science', which would lend support to the view that, by 1930, archaeologists were beginning to be regarded, or possibly to regard themselves, as superior to antiquarians or antiquaries, the distinction being between scientists and dabblers. At the present time, 'antiquarian' is certainly a pejorative term. To label someone an 'antiquarian' implies quite clearly that he is being written off.

It is important to notice, however, that at no point does the *Oxford English Dictionary* equate 'archaeologist' with 'excavator'. It does not even suggest 'excavator' as one of several possible meanings of 'archaeologist'. Whatever the feelings of archaeologists themselves may have ben at this time, they are not reflected in the *Dictionary*. In this connection, it is amusing and possibly significant to observe that in his immensely successful *Ur of the Chaldees*, published in 1929, Sir Leonard Woolley does not use the words 'archaeology' or 'archaeologist' even once.

The *Oxford English Dictionary*, of necessity, does no more than record the history and meaning of words like other dictionaries. It offers few clues as to what proportion of what kinds of English people used or understood a particular word at a particular time. One might guess that in, say, 1880, very few English people would have known what archaeology was, but this would be a pure guess. A century later, however, one can be quite sure, simply by asking a direct question, that a majority of one's fellow citizens do have at least a vague idea as to what archaeology is and one knows, too, that they believe it is connected with digging up the past. Since archaeology does not mean only digging up the past, one is entitled to feel that those who have devoted so much time and energy to popularising archaeology have either been very one-sided in their propaganda, which is true, or have been seriously misunderstood, which is also true.

Since most misunderstandings, disagreements and quarrels are caused by some degree of semantic vagueness, it may be helpful to compare the views of one or two well-known and influential archaeologists as to what archaeology actually is.

We could usefully begin with Margaret Murray, who lived to be a hundred and whose acquaintance with archaeologists was exceptionally wide and who had had more than the usual number of years in which to pursue ideas to a satisfactory conclusion. For her, 'archaeology is the whole history of man's advance, mentally and spiritually, from the time of his emergence from the animal as a true human being until the present day'.[3] 'Archaeology and anthropology,' she went on, 'have one end in view, the study of the human being, archaeology dealing with the development, anthropology with the end product.'[4]

It is an interesting point of view, although Dr Murray's distinction between archaeology and anthropology is not, perhaps, quite as clear as it might be. What matters, however, is that for her archaeology is and must be essentially an humane study, aimed at understanding how man developed and how he learned how to come to terms with his environment. Sir Leonard Woolley was very much of her way of thinking. 'The real end of archaeology,' he gradually came to understand, 'is, through the dead-and-gone things, to get at the history and minds of dead-and-gone men.'[5]

O. G. S. Crawford's view was that 'archaeology is merely the past tense of anthropology',[6] which expresses in a slightly different way Margaret Murray's opinion, that anthropologists study man as he is now, archaeologists man as he used to be. For Crawford, archaeology is concerned with 'past phases of human culture', and the basis of culture, he insisted, is technology. A good archaeologist must be interested in and knowledgeable about every aspect of the culture he has chosen to study, its technology, its social organisation, its political system. Otherwise, he cannot interpret what he finds, he cannot talk sense. Crawford was greatly influenced by the writings and friendship of Gordon Childe and agreed with Childe that the essence of archaeology is a concern with the development of the human race and of the various forms of civilisation which it has evolved.

It is not helpful, however, to equate archaeologists with excavators. The two tasks are different, although very occasionally the same person may have the temperament and the ability to carry out both equally well. In general, however, there is good reason to agree with the judegement of J. N. L. Myres, one-time President of the Society of Antiquaries. 'It is certainly not the case,' Myres believed, 'that all genuine archaeologists must have mastered the techniques required for a modern excavation. There are many excellent archaeologists who have no taste for digging.'[7] He might have added that there are many excellent excavators who have no taste for interpretation and no particular skill in that direction. Archaeology, however, needs both its interpreters and its excavators. There is a parallel situation to be found in television, where the producer, the creative person, the man or woman who conceives the idea of a programme and who guides and controls its progress through to the finished product, has a different function and quite possibly a different group of talents from the director, who supervises the practical aspects of the programme, as an intermediary between the producer and the technicians.

The bigger an archaeological project is, the more necessary it becomes to acknowledge this division of labour and to plan for it. Consider, for example, exactly what is implied in the first few lines of one of Martin Biddle's reports on his great excavation project at Winchester. The year in question was 1969, the excavation lasted for fourteen weeks and the average number of people taking part at any given time was 170.

> The City of Winchester and King Alfred's College provided the necessary hostel accommodation. The Army supplied cooks and hostel equipment and the City Engineer, Mr. L. M. Perkis, and the City Architect, Mr. C, Steptoe, arranged for the adaptation and maintenance of the buildings. The Warden and Deputy Warden, Mr. and Mrs. Geoffrey Heald, ran a very large camp with precision and drive, yet with kindness and accessibility, serving 23,168 meals in the course of the season. The Hospitality Committee, through Mr. Neville Barker, Mr. Frank Cottrill, and Mr. John Dockerill, ran tours and other facilities for volunteers. As in the previous season, my secretary, Miss Caroline Raison, made all the arrangements concerning volunteers and I am very grateful for her help in all the necessary administration.[8]

Raising funds for the excavation was a major task in itself. £23,000 was spent during the season and this came from many sources.

> The Excavations Committee is most grateful to the following bodies for their generous financial support: the Old Dominion Foundation through the University of North Carolina and Duke University, the Ministry of Public Building and Works, the Hampshire Country Council, the City of Winchester, the British Academy, the British Museum, the Society of

Antiquaries, and many private donors. A valuable contribution to the available funds came from the donations and publications sales resulting from guided tours of the site organised by Mr. F. C. Mallett, Assistant Secretary of the Excavations Committee, and carried through by himself, by student volunteers from the sites, and by a devoted band of local residents.[9]

The work-force had an international character to it. 'Some 335 volunteers from this country and from the Commonwealth, from the United States, and from most European countries took part in the excavation, under the guidance of about forty site-supervisors and technical assistants.'[10]

All this amounts to saying that Mr Biddle was in command of a private army, with its General Staff, Liaison Officers, Battalion and Platoon Commanders and supporting specialists of all kinds, from the Catering Corps to the Engineers. An excavation on this scale cannot be carried out without first-class organisation and close attention to the most prosaic details and in this sense Martin Biddle was a distinguished and highly successful member of the body of great archaeologist-generals, which has included Sir Leonard Woolley, Professor Leslie Alcock, Sir Flinders Petrie and, of course, that very military figure, Sir Mortimer Wheeler himself.

But it is probably more rewarding from the point of view of the present book to consider the information provided by Martin Biddle in civilian terms, because it is an admirable illustration of the place which archaeology has come to occupy in Britain during the past half century, of it social implications. The Winchester project was planned and organised in a typically British way. First, once the decision to have the excavation had been taken, a Committee was set up to make the local arrangements and to raise funds. It was composed of competent, energetic and influential people, who carried out both their tasks with great efficiency and in this way relieved the Director of many worries, some of a major kind, some merely tedious and time-consuming, leaving him relatively free to concentrate on the professional aspects of the excavation. The necessary money and practical support were obtained, as the list shows, from what one might call the usual British mixture of private and public sources – the local authority, the relevant Ministry, museums and professional bodies, industrial and commercial concerns, charitable trusts and private individuals, by no means all of whom could be described as rich. A far from insignificant amount was raised on and around the site, on a day to day basis, by the well-established technique of rattling the collecting box in front of people who had been interested in what was going on and by selling them souvenirs of their visit while they were in a receptive and generous mood. The showmanship involved in presenting a project of this kind to the public is a very professional affair and an important part of the success of the whole venture. The fact that the dig was in a place like Winchester was extremely helpful. During the summer months the city receives a large number of tourists from all over the world. The audience, the customers and the donors are ready to hand, in their thousands every week.

But, even in the 1960s, before inflation began to be the financial and social disaster it has since become – the serious effects of inflation on archaeology will be explored later – the figure of £23,000 for the whole costs of a fourteen-week excavation was extremely modest. It was possible to keep the budget within these limits only by attracting unpaid labour, the enthusiasts euphemistically and charmingly referred to in Britain as volunteers, an untranslatable word. These people, mostly of student age, came, as the Director emphasised, from all over the world, and each year there were more than three hundred of them, all needing to be housed and fed, kept interested and contented and organised in such a way as to be effective workers.

The volunteer labour corps employed each year on archaeological sites in Britain has never been studied with the care it deserves. When this is eventually done, as it must surely be one day, it will be revealed as a remarkable social phenomenon. During the digging season, for the past thirty years at least, a God's-eye view of the British Isles would show a considerable number of archaeological excavations and surveys in progress, mainly manned by volunteers and run on a shoe-string. The pattern for the Continent has, in general, been quite different, with far fewer operations in progress at any given time, a much greater reliance on public funds, and a much smaller use of unpaid labour. The consequences of this difference have been profound. One could go as far as to say that it is the widespread use of volunteers which has given archaeology in Britain its special, unique, democratic quality. People who come for love of the subject, who receive no payment and who are free to leave whenever they feel inclined have to be treated as equals, not as coolies. On a British site, the autocrat will usually fail, unless the people he employs have some very good professional reason for deciding to put up with his whims.

At Winchester, as we have mentioned, there were about forty site-supervisors and technical assistants. Of these, social historians will be interested to observe, sixteen were women. The proportion of women to men in archaeological excavations in Britain is frequently a good deal higher than this. Archaeology, like pony clubs, is in a fair way to becoming a distinctly feminine pursuit, for reasons which will be discussed in a later chapter. At the moment, it seems necessary to say only that the fact may be of some social and psychological importance.

But, sex apart, the total of forty supervisors and technicians deserves our attention. It can be subdivided into approximately thirty supervisors and ten technicians. Let us concentrate on the thirty supervisors. These are the charge-hands, the foremen, the middle management of archaeology, the people who are responsible for making sure that the work is carried out properly and who provide the Director with detailed reports of exactly what has happened and what has been discovered in their particular section of the work. It is from their reports that the Director will eventually write his overall description of the site and his assessment of its significance. Their competence and accuracy is crucial.

What Winchester therefore presents to us is archaeology on four levels. At Level A, the bottom of the pyramid of archaeological interest and involvement, there is the general public, visiting the site, reading about it, looking at it on television, talking to friends about it and, in a small way, subscribing to its funds. Level B consists of what one might call the Supporters' Club, that is, the Excavation Committee, the Hospitality Committee, the people who ran the camp, organised the volunteers and the outings, and made the major contributions to the funds. Level C comprised the volunteer workers, learning more about archaeological techniques and, in many cases, about Britain and having a pleasant holiday in the open air at no cost to themselves. At Level D, the apex of the pyramid, were the professionals – General Biddle and his staff of supervisors and technicians.

The whole pyramid, from top to bottom, forms the entity which is entitled to carry the label, 'Archaeology in Britain'. Each level depends for its existence and functioning on the other three, but the people whom one could fairly describe as archaeologists are to be found only on Levels C and D. The ways in which this situation has come about form the theme and the subject matter of the chapters which follow. The pace of development, however, has been very uneven. What was happening in 1930 was not greatly different from what was happening in 1910 or 1900. Between the outbreak of war in 1939 and the early 1950s, archaeology, like most other activities, stagnated. It took a long time to recover from the war, but once activity really got going again it soon became evident that, during the twenty-year slumber, British archaeology had shed many of its traditional habits. The scale, the methods of financing, the social context, the techniques and equipment, the personnel and the philosophy had all undergone radical changes.

The best summary of what happened during the half century following the First World War is to be found in the Presidential Address delivered to the Society of Antiquaries on the hundredth aniversary of its move to Burlington House in 1875.

When I was an undergraduate more than fifty years ago, persons who could be properly described as professional archaeologists were very rare birds indeed. A few posts in two or three departments of the British Museum, one or two more in the National Museums of Scotland and Wales and in university museums, then almost confined to Oxford and Cambridge, two or perhaps three professorships, none of them with any departmental staff, and a minimal number of very badly paid posts in the Royal Commissions and the Ancient Monuments Inspectorate of H.M. Office of Works. Finally, of course, there was our late Fellow, O. G. S. Crawford, who had just forced himself as a more or less self-appointed Archaeology Officer upon a reluctant and somewhat resentful Ordnance Survey. That was about the lot, and, even if one includes the more or less learned Secretaries of three of four learned Societies and the Directors of the British Schools in Athens and Rome, the total number of scholars who could be properly described as professional archaeologists at that time was probably no more than twenty-five or thirty at the outside. When I inquired, on taking my degree, about the prospects of archaeology as a career, I was firmly warned off by my mentors, for all practical purposes, I was told, there were no careers in archaeology, and, if one had to earn a living, as I had, one must find some other way of doing it.[11]

This did not mean, as Dr Myres pointed out, that archaeology was a non-subject or that excellent work and a great deal of work was not being done on it. But it was being carried out for the most part by people who were able to make an income in other ways. They were university teachers in history or classics, schoolmasters, lawyers, doctors, clergymen and so on.

One may well wonder if this was or is always a bad thing. Is a job necessarily done better by people who spend their whole time doing it? Most Victorians would probably have said no, but fashions have changed, and the Age of Professionalism has decreed that the more university chairs and full-time experts of all kinds of subject has, the more important and finance-worthy that subject must be, the implication being that research is proceeding at such a pace and knowledge is all the time accumulating in such a mountainous fashion that only a person who is in the position to devote twelve months a year, seven days a week to the study and practice of a subject can have any chance of keeping himself fully informed and up-to-date.

Even if this assumption is false, there are obviously great advantages for suitably qualified people in search of jobs if those in a position to create and offer jobs can be persuaded that it is true. The major fallacy is so rarely stated that no harm can be done by revealing it now. It is, as observation and experience make sadly clear, that many so-called professionals are idle, make little attempt to renew their knowledge and contribute remarkably little to the advancement of what they are content to call their subject. This is no more and no less true of archaeologists than of other kinds of people. It is simply a fact of life and it would be extremely surprising if archaeologists were to be an exception to the general rule.

The interesting fact is that a great many people put much more energy and interest into their spare-time occupations than into the work by which they earn a living; and both scholarship and the community are the richer for what, at least in theory, is no doubt a regrettable state of affairs. But, after the 1939–45 war, for one reason and another, the excavators, who had made a number of take-over bids for archaeology, began a determined campaign to win some kind of professional status for themselves. Paradoxically, this coincided with a great increase in the popular appeal of archaeology and the two were almost certainly connected. The more archaeologists, or some of them, became well-known public figures, the more eager they became to be thought of as professionals, with the cashet that involves.

J. N. L. Myres puts the point – and it is of great importance – in the following way:

> Archaeology passed almost overnight from being the part-time pre-occupation of a few specialists and amateurs, to become a subject with a very great popular appeal which under the skilful guidance of a few of our more distinguished Fellows, soon began to exert a considerable force in public life. It is the culmination of this process which we are now witnessing in the current controversy over the place of professionalism in archaeology.[12]

The situation is a difficult one and it has its roots in the way in which archaeology in Britain has developed over more than two centuries and in the great variety of people who have contributed to that development. For these reasons, the struggle to create anything amounting to an archaeological profession may well prove to be largely futile. Whatever the position may be on the Continent, both East and West of the Iron Curtain, archaeology here is now so broadly based and covers such a wide range of historical interests that any thorough-going attempt to create a closed shop, which is what professionalism amounts to, will almost certainly fail. Tradition is against it, and Myres' analysis and championship of the British tradition in this field cannot be improved upon. He observes:

> Archaeologists have not in the past been subjected to the unifying forces which a common educational background or vocational training have provided for the practitioners of other professions.[13] Our leading archaeologists have sprung from every sort of origin: university courses of all kinds, mainly perhaps in classics and history, but with a sprinkling of scientists, engineers, laywers, philosophers, orientalists or theologians. Many have come direct from the practice of other professions, from schoolmastering, medicine, architecture or the Civil Service. Others again, with no strictly adademic antecedents, have been businessmen, bankers or laboratory technicians. Closely allied to this wide variety of backgrounds has been the powerful tradition of amateurism in British archaeology.[14]

What Myres calls 'the powerful tradition of amateurism' might also be termed 'the powerful tradition of well-spent leisure'. Archaeology, like science and sport, owes a great deal to people who, because they could live on inherited money, had no need to work, which is another way of saying that for the whole of the nineteenth century and a substantial part of the twentieth, archaeology was largely an upper-class and upper-middle-class pursuit. Many members of these two layers of British society did have occupations, sometimes from necessity, sometimes from choice, but their work as clergymen, professors, doctors, merchants, soldiers and lawyers usually allowed them a great deal of spare time and surplus energy with which to follow other interests.

It was, as we shall see in Chapter One, these people who founded and supported the many societies which sprang up in Victorian times as focal points for people who had developed or inherited an interest in the British past. Their concern was with archaeology in the broadest sense – churches, barrows, country houses, tombs, heraldry, brasses, Roman remains, armour and weapons, battles and craftsmanship – and without them the modern concept and practice of archaeology would not have the popular appeal which has been invaluable during the great growth period of the past thirty years.

But, precisely because so many people and so many different kinds of people are involved in archaeology today, the battle over the definition of the word is, as Myres saw, crucial. It is not at all simply a matter of splitting hairs. What archaeology is faced with is a determined attempt on the part of some of the most influential excavators, individually and in unison, to equate archaeology with excavation. It would be disastrous for all concerned, the excavators included, if this attempt should succeed. It is well to understand the roots of the campaign and, for diplomatic reasons, to use the words of the President of the Society of Antiquaries rather than one's own. He says as his first point:

> There is now a growing body of practitioners whose claim to be professional archaeologists rests wholly or mainly on their skill in the techniques of excavation and on their managerial competence in all the ways that are nowadays required for the efficient conduct of a dig. Such people are coming to form a considerable force, largely dependent on the increasing provision of public funds, whether central or local, for their livelihood. . . . They inevitably come to regard the practice of excavation as the essence of the matter and are concerned that skill and experience in this field should receive proper professional recognition, quite apart from any contributions to the advancement of knowledge that may result from their operations.[15]

And, secondly

> . . . even among the many societies which have sprung up during the past hundred years for the specialised study of particular periods or aspects of antiquity, it will be found that the hard core of the membership, which alone keeps them financially viable, normally consists not of professionals earning their living by the practice of those particular disciplines but of a broad mass of generally interested amateurs drawn from many walks of life. And it is, moreover, normally the case that much of the more significant work being done in these specialised fields is being done by non-professionals, as a glance through any of our learned journals will show.[16]

What Myres says is indisputable. It is the remarkable and, on the whole, very happy mixture of amateurs and professionals which has given British archaeology its special value and character and which has enabled it to accomplish so much. The cross-fertilisation of ideas which has always existed in the national and local societies devoted to archaeology has been of the greatest benefit to the experts and the merely interested alike. It has kept the subject alive and, incidentally, made it much easier to survive economic and political changes.

The truth is, and one might as well say this bluntly, that the people who appear to be so anxious to achieve what they call professional status are nearly always people who feel in one way or another insecure. Without the professional label, they are never sure about their niche in society and they are always liable to feel that their work is not receiving adequate public recognition. This craving for status is much more likely to occur among people who, as a result of their intelligence, education and possibly good fortune, have been able to rise socially and to achieve something barred to their parents, a skilled middle-class occupation. They require some form of public acknowledgement that the job is important – income alone is not sufficient for this – and, equally essential, a guarantee that funds will continue to be available to finance it. A job is socially expendable, a profession is clearly something that society needs. This yearning to be considered professional is not, of course, peculiar to archaeologists. It is very marked among, for example, teachers and museum staffs and always for the same reasons.

Paradoxically, the confirmed 'amateurs' – the word is very inadequate and misleading – seem to feel much more secure than the would-be professionals, mainly, one suspects, because their bread-winning function gives them the social position they expect and require. But there is more to the problem than this. Because they come to archaeology, as it were from outside, the amateurs are often in a better position to keep the mechanics of the subject, the technology, in its place. By identifying archaeology with excavating, the excavators do both themselves and archaeology a bad turn, because they downgrade the meaning of the word 'archaeology'. The highest grade of archaeologist is that rare person who has the ability to see the wood for the trees, to interpret discoveries and to fit them into a broad historical and cultural pattern. The excavator, for all his professional skills, is often unable to do this. So the essential practical work at Winchester was carried out, with great competence, by the hundreds of volunteers and the forty supervisors and technicians – the excavators – but the reports which made sense of it all came from the brain and the imagination of the Director, Martin Biddle.

A highly developed historical imagination is a scarce gift, but the progress of archaeology depends entirely on its availability. Without it, the technical advances are pointless and worthless, mere tools with which nothing can be made. Once this is understood and admitted, the claims of the excavators to be or to become 'the profession' are seen to be ridiculous. What profession? Nobody would dream of advocating anything as mundane as 'the excavating profession', a fact which gives the show away. Only 'archaeology' has the prestige. It is the essential status word, especially for those who are without the superior intelligence and the poetic insight which are the prerogative of the highest grade of archaeologist.

This book, then, is unconcerned with heresies, taboos and unconventional thinking. It asks not only who the archaeologists and their helpers were, but what their background was and what motivated them. It tries to place the archaeological knights and squires within the society of their time and to discover what society thought of them.

1 The Victorians and their Societies

In 1949 the Somersetshire Archaeological and Natural History Society celebrated its centenary. At its first Annual Meeting, in Taunton, 'about 350 people were present and an adjoining room was fitted up as a temporary museum.' It is interesting to notice that, in explaining the Society's aims and range of interests, the Chairman of the inaugural meeting, Sir Walter Trevelyan, referred first to natural history, then to architecture – Roman and medieval – and then to family and parish records. The emphasis was not on archaeology, in today's fashionable and restricted sense of the term, but on what we now describe as the environment, a trendy word which the Victorians never used in this sense. This concept of the country as a natural and cultural unit was of great importance to the Victorians and it has taken us the best part of a century to find our way back to the perspective and the truth it embodies. The environmental archaeologists of the 1970s are thinking and behaving in a good Victorian fashion, although most of them write and talk as if they had discovered a fundamentally new approach.

At the 1849 meeting the principal speaker was Dr William Buckland, 'the learned and witty Dean of Westminster', who spoke on *Somerset Geology* and showed how it had influenced the places and peoples of the County. Buckland had been a Devon rector and throughout his life remained an enthusiastic amateur naturalist and geologist. His scientific interests had resulted in his election to a Fellowship of the Royal Society in 1818. His son, Frank, was one of the most distinguished of Victorian naturalists, who had a life of extraordinary variety and richness. He trained as a doctor at St George's Hospital; spent his long vacations working in Liebig's laboratory at Giessen; served as a surgeon in the Life Guards, mainly because he needed the money; wrote for *The Field* and eventually became her Majesty's inspector of salmon fisheries. With a different father, he could very easily have included archaeology among his activities. The family atmosphere encouraged a comprehensive view of the development of man and his surroundings, and archaeology formed part of this.

One particular paragraph in Dr Buckland's address to the newly formed Somerset Society is a perfect example of the Victorian instinct for ignoring the dividing lines between one academic subject and another and for regarding knowledge and enlightenment as a whole. Dr Buckland firmly believed that the geology of a region and the characteristics of its inhabitants were closely related.

> The existence of such towns as Bath, Wells and Taunton, in the richest valleys, and the non-existence of any towns at all upon the tops of Quantock, or Blackdown, or Exmoor, depend upon geological causes. Why were the meadows of Bridgwater and the rich marsh lands of Somerset so productive of fat cattle and well-fed inhabitants? – Why was the Vale of Taunton favoured so much before all other localities in – I might say almost in the whole world? – Why that full and perfect development of the human species both male and female? When travelling over Europe in 1820 with a German Geologist more observant than myself, whenever we came to a town where there were more pretty faces than usual, he would say – 'We are coming to a good geological formation' – And the moment we got into the mountain regions – the Also, for instance – ugliness was the universal characteristic.[1]

Most unfortunately, during the second half of the nineteenth century, the Society, like most of its contemporaries,[2] gradually subordinated natural history to archaeology. Its Ornithological, Botanical and Geological Sections continued to exist, but increasingly as poor relations, although during the 1960s and 1970s of the present century they have experienced a welcome revival and renewal of confidence, as what we had better call Environmentalism gathers ground. There is good reason to believe that the lesser position which natural history came to occupy in the Society's affairs – and this was entirely typical of what was happening over the country as a whole – was the result of becoming more specialised and more popular. The first trend made the subject, or rather group of subjects, seem beyond the reach of the majority of the Society's members and the second converted it into something that had too much the appearance of a mere hobby, suitable for field clubs and schools, but not for serious-minded members of the middle-class.

What should be given particular prominence in the history of the Somerset Society, and of most of its fellow societies with similar aims, was the attention paid to organising excursions, and to their popularity. One of the greatest achievements of these societies was in getting their members and friends out into the countryside and the villages, where they could see history for themselves, in its natural setting. In the nineteenth century, before the advent of cars and coaches, this was not an easy thing to arrange. Parties found their way to the nearest railway station – Somerset had a poor railway service – and then either walked or went by some form of horse-drawn transport. Despite all the difficulties, it was not at all exceptional to attract a hundred or more people to one of these historical excursions.

2. *Robert Munro, F.S.A., died 1920* (p. 23).
'*A few years later his resources were such as to free him from his arduous professional labours, and with his interest steadily fixed on the aspect of the subject which had primarily attracted him, he retired from his practice and devoted himself henceforth entirely to archaeology.*'

But this, as the Somerset Society's 1949 President, Sir Arthur Hobhouse, pointed out during the Centenary celebrations, was a period in which individual initiative and a certain amount of effort and hardship were taken for granted.

> Those were the days when there was great enthusiasm for learning, scientific discovery and records of the past. There was no Office of Works to take over the preservation of ancient buildings, no National Trust to hold places of historic interest and natural beauty, no local authority with power to collect deeds and documents of the past or to spend money on museums, and no state education system to stimulate interest in the study of nature. Whatever was done 100 years ago in this direction was left to private persons.[3]

Sir Arthur Hobhouse's own family was a reasonably typical example of these 'private persons', who regarded it as their duty – in many instances it was their pleasure as well – to support the county archaeological and agricultural societies. At the first Annual General Meeting in 1849, Sir Arthur's grandfather, the Right Hon. Henry Hobhouse, P.C, was appointed a Vice-President; his career in the public service had included holding the office of Keeper of the State Papers from 1826 until his death in 1854. Bishop Edmund Hobhouse, who died in 1904, was an eminent local historian. Sir Arthur's father, the Right Hon. Henry Hobhouse, P.C, served as President in 1890 and again in 1913. The 1850 Annual Report had good reason to record that its list of 250 subscribing members included 'a very good proportion of our principal landed proprietors and literary men'.

Membership lists are sometimes misleading – they give little clue to the age and income of members, for example – but, interpreted with a certain amount of caution, they give a reasonable impression of the kind of people who found it worth their while to join the society in question and, if one compares the lists over a long period of time, one certainly sees how the character of the membership has changed. Suppose, for instance, that one works out, for any given year, the percentage of members who were titled, doctors, Army or Navy officers, women or clergymen. The figures for the three years of the Bristol and Gloucestershire Archaeological Society are as follows:

	1876[4]	1900	1930
Titled	3.6	3.6	7.2
Doctors	2.9	1.6	0.4
Army or Navy	8.1	4.4	7.2
Clergymen	20.3	14.9	3.8
Women	1.9	6.8	22.3

The apparent rise in the proportion of titled people between 1900 and 1930 is not quite what it seems. It is accounted for mainly by the appearance in the 1930 list of a number of titled ladies and, as such, forms part of the overall and remarkable rise in the percentage of women among the subscribers to the Society.

The decreasing number of doctors is possibly a result of the changing nature and pattern of the profession, with medicine becoming a more scientific affair, with fewer attractions for men of broad interests. It could also reflect the growing importance of Bristol and Gloucester as medical centres, with more doctors concentrated in these places and relatively fewer in the villages and small towns, where they were the lay equivalent of the vicar, with considerable leisure to devote to their spare-time interests.

The fall in the proportion of Army and Navy officers between 1876 and 1900 is difficult to explain, but the remarkably high figure for 1930 was probably caused by the habit, especially strong in rural society, of holding on to the military title one acquired during the 1914–18 War. At no date, however, is it possible to distinguish between officers who have retired and officers who are still serving except by the region's method of consulting the Army and Navy lists for each year. The probability is, however, that the majority of the Service people who figure in these lists had retired from active duties.

It will be noticed that the percentage of clergymen in 1876 is almost exactly the same as the percentage of women in 1930. The two sets of figures have changed places. When one speaks of clergymen in this context, it is almost invariably Church of England clergymen who are meant. The Roman Catholic and Nonconformist clergy have played a very small part in the activities of local archaeological societies, partly because, until recent times, they have had to work harder than their Church of England colleagues, partly because they had less money to spare, but mainly, no doubt, because they operated within a different tradition. But what has happened to the Church of England clergy is quite another matter. There are, to begin with, far fewer of them than there were a hundred years ago. This process was well under way in the 1930s, already it has greatly accelerated since 1945. Parishes have been amalgamated on a large scale, and the kind of rural parson who was plentiful at one time, the man with a private income, a small village church and very little to do, is now a very rare bird indeed. So too, alas, is the vicar of a scholarly turn of mind who used his vicarage and his living as a heaven-sent opportunity to read and write. The scholarly clergyman was one of the mainstays of the county archaeology society until at least the outbreak of the First World War. One in five of the Bristol and Gloucestershire members were in Holy Orders, and the percentage elsewhere was very similar.

The spectacular rise in the number of women members of all the county societies is not merely a product of the feminist movement, although that naturally had something to do with it. Among the other factors which probably contributed to this remarkable change in the social pattern were the reduction in the number of children a woman had to bear; the improvement in women's health and the increase in longevity, partly due to their smaller families and partly to more sensible living habits; the growing fashion for outdoor exercise; the rise in the number of motorcars and the steady improvement in their reliability; and the considerable increase in the number of women who had received some form of higher education. The First World War made it necessary for many more middle-class women to play an active part in public life and this change continued and developed during the 1920s and 1930s.

But, in the case of archaeology – or what was thought of as archaeology – there was another cause. Very few women have ever been interested in political or military history, which some would hold to be evidence of their good sense, and so long as history was reckoned to be confined to these aspects of the past it remained virtually a male preserve. Over the past hundred years, however, two new kinds of history, social and local history, gradually became more respectable and therefore more popular. The archaeological societies did a great deal to encourage this revolution, often withour realising exactly what was happening or what the revolution was really about. Local records, genealogy, houses, churches, castles, furniture, hill-forts and ruins of all kinds were the raw material from which the archaeological societies created their programmes and around which they constructed their excursions. What was happening was an interest in the kind of lives our ancestors, some of them very remote, lived, a wish to use one's imagination to recreate past life-styles.

One should not exaggerate the speed with which historical thinking and awareness changed. As anyone who was at school during the 1920s or 1930s will remember very well, history at that time still consisted overwhelmingly of battles, treaties, kings and queens and political intriguing and manoeuvring. It was the publication of Trevelyan's *English Social History* in 1942, in the middle of the war, which began to tailor political history down to size and to suggest what few previous historians had dared to say or even think, that the common people were part of history. The Victorians did not get quite as far as this, but some of them certainly reached the first stage, believing that social history in general was interesting, especially when it concerned the families of the governing classes, and that local history had distinct possibilities. And archaeology, in any case, was a very impressive and respectable-sounding word.

At the centre of the national life, in London, the situation was rather different from what it was in the provinces. An analysis of the membership of the Society of Antiquaries reveals rather a different pattern from what is to be found in the records of the Bristol and Gloucestershire Society. The proportion of women is negligible and there are far fewer doctors and military men.

	1900	*1930*
Titled	9.9	8.8
Doctors	1.6	1.9
Army or Navy	1.9	8.0
Clergymen	12.7	7.0
Women	0.2	0.7

One cannot, of course, make a direct comparison between the membership of the Society of Antiquaries and the membership of a county archaeological society, since the first is the result of election and the second is, broadly speaking, open to anyone of good repute who is willing and able to pay the subscription. It may come as something of a surprise, even so, to discover a higher proportion of titled people among the Antiquaries and, even in 1930, such a tiny proportion of women of sufficient eminence in the historical/architectural/archaeological fields to be felt worthy of election.

For at least the period up to the beginning of the First World War, one has, in fact, to regard archaeology on the national level, if membership of the Society of Antiquaries can be taken to represent that level, as a wholly male subject, and probably the best way of illustrating the kind of men involved is to select from the obituaries published in the *Antiquaries Journal*. This has the double advantage of outlining their backgrounds, their careers, and their interests and of indicating what their peers and contemporaries thought about them, always allowing for the mellowness and kindness which is normal in an obituary notice at any period.

All these people were born between 1835 and 1870, so that at least some part of their working life fell within the nineteenth century. They are presented here in the order of the date of their birth. A few foreign Fellows have been included, as a way of throwing the British type into sharper relief.

1834
Bishop George Forrest Browne[5] d. 1930

'The death of Bishop Browne,' said the *Journal*, 'removes a great archaeologist, whose working life has been prolonged far beyond the ordinary limit.'

He wrote a number of books, and 'this voluminous work may be said to have been partly the cause and partly the effect of his holding the position of Disney Professor of Archaeology in the University of Cambridge from 1887 to 1892. Other archaeologists did not agree with his conclusions, but they were formed after close study and, though often expressed dogmatically,

3. Mill Stephenson, F.S.A., died 1937 (on left of picture).
'Spared from the necessity of having to earn his living, he was able to devote his boundless energy throughout practically the whole of his long life to the pursuit of those antiquarian studies in which he was interested.' (pp. 31–2.)

were always provocative of thought and further study. They were stimulating to a degree, and must have attracted to the study of history and archaeology many who usually took no note of such things.'

He was elected a Fellow of the Society of Antiquaries in 1888. 'In the *Antiquaries Journal* emphasis must naturally be laid on archaeology, but it would be absurd to call Bishop Browne an antiquary only.'

'For many years he was a great figure in the University of Cambridge. His regular work was that of Secretary of the Local Examinations and Lectures Syndicate, which included both branches of the University's extra-mural work. Bishop Browne was equally concerned with the internal administration of the University, and, for many years, was Secretary of the Council of Senate.'

1835
Robert Munro[6] d. 1920

Munroe was born in Ross-shire and qualified as a doctor at the University of Edinburgh. 'After taking his medical degree, he settled down in a practice in Kilmarnock, and for a space of about twenty years led the life of a busy and successful country practitioner. When in 1877 the Ayrshire and Galloway Archaeological Society was formed, Dr Munro became one of the original members, and having previously had his attention arrested when on the Continent by the display of relics from the Swiss lake dwellings, responded immediately to an invitation to help in the excavation of Crannogs in Ayrshire undertaken by that Society under the leadership of Mr Cochran Patrick. His zeal grew with the widening of the field of exploration, and in time Munro became the leader of the enterprise and in 1882 published the results of his researches in the volume entitled *Scottish Lake Dwellings*.

'A few years later his resources were such as to free him from his arduous professional labours, and with his interest steadily fixed on the aspect of the subject which had primarily attracted him, he retired from his practice and devoted himself henceforth entirely to archaeology. To make himself conversant with continental analogies, he indulged his taste for travel, and in 1888, on the invitation of the Society of Antiquaries of Scotland, he delivered a course of Rhind lectures, taking as his subject, *The Lake Dwellings of Europe*. These lectures, illustrated by the skilful draughtsmanship of his wife, were published in book form in 1890, and appeared in a French edition in 1908. The merit of the volume was clearly recognised and gave its author a wide reputation.'

In 1893 he became President of the Anthropological Section of the British Association and in the following year he was appointed Chairman of the Committee to supervise the excavation of the Glastonbury lake village. He endowed an annual course of lectures at the University of Edinburgh on Anthropology and Prehistoric Archaeology and in 1910, at the age of 75, he delivered the first course himself. The Universities of Edinburgh and Glasgow both awarded him an honorary doctorate.

'As an archaeologist, Munro was eminently sane and reliable, and his methods, due no doubt to his professional training, thoroughly scientific. To his other qualities may be added an absorbing enthusiasm and a sense of good fellowship by which he will be kindly thought of by those who enjoyed the privilege of his friendship.'

1842
William Gowland[7] d. 1922

Gowland studied at the Royal School of Mines, became Head of the Japanese Mint and in 1905 was appointed Professor of Metallurgy at the Imperial College of Science and Technology. He was elected a Fellow of the Royal Society in 1909. He also served as President of the Institute of Metals and of the Royal Anthropological Institute.

In 1895 he was elected a Fellow of the Society of Antiquaries and became one of its Vice-Presidents in 1902. He wrote extensively on early metallurgy and 'his knowledge of chemistry and of mineralogy was of great service to the Society.'

1842
Sir Henry Howarth[8] d. 1923

He was born in Lisbon, where his father was in business. He studied law at the Inner Temple, 'but the practice of his profession did not attract him so much as politics, nor as much as history and science. He became M.P. for Salford, wrote a *History of the Mongols* and was in due course elected a Fellow of the Society of Antiquaries.

'It is the fashion now to make the age an age of specialists, but Sir Henry Howarth did not conform to that fashion. He was rather of those who, like Bacon, take all knowledge for their province, and so he was often able to suggest analogies between one subject and another which would not occur to the specialist, and it may be that much of the usefulness of his contributions to knowledge is to be traced to this fact. The fact, too, that he had so many interests may also explain the extraordinary freshness of his mind to the end of his eighty-one years.'

Sir Henry was, in short, a man with a breadth of interests much more normal in Victorian times, and which fortunately included archaeology.

1843
John William Legg[9] d. 1922

After studying medicine, Legg practised as a doctor until 1883, when illness forced him to retire. He devoted the rest of his long life to studying liturgy and was the inspirer and real founder, in 1890, of the Henry Bradshaw Society for Editing Rare Liturgical Texts.

'His scientific training was invaluable to him in his new work, and his writings were marked by a critical accuracy which demolished many errors.'

'He would not allow his friends to call him a learned man, and he expressed surprise that the University of Oxford should deem his work worthy of an honorary Doctorate of Letters, but he was by instinct, as well as by training and achievement, a scholar and a man of learning. His knowledge was not only deep but wide, and far from being restricted to the limits of his published writings. He could have lectured on many periods of history and literature, for he read much and forgot little.'

'His home was happy and hospitable, and he gave unsparingly to his guests from the shores of his knowledge, his wit, and his reminiscences.'

1843
Professor Oscar Montelius[10] d. 1922

Director of the Historical Museum, Stockholm, and State Antiquary, Professor Montelius was no ordinary man and one whom the Society was proud to include among its Fellows.

'In every sense, he was a giant – in stature, in scope and output, in his power of minute analysis combined with the broadest outlook, and above all his gift for tongues. He could, and often did, address scientific meetings in English, French or German almost as fluently and correctly as in his mother tongue; and his knowledge of several other languages enabled him to collect and utilise an enormous amount of European material which is or will be rendered available in a series of volumes, superbly illustrated, and published largely at his own expense. It may be easily imagined that he was always one of the most striking and popular figures at international Congresses, where he will be sadly missed.

1844
Harold Arthur, 17th Viscount Dillon[11] d. 1932

A great authority on armour and weapons, Lord Dillon was Curator, from 1892 to 1913, of the Armouries at the Tower of London, where 'he reduced the chaotic historical innacuracies which had grown up during more than a quarter of a century'. He undertook an immense list of public duties during his very long life, being at various times President of the Royal Archaeological Institute, a Trustee of the British Museum, Wallace Collection and the National Portrait Gallery.

'He was well-known, not only in this country, but in the antiquarian world at large, as a student and authority of the first order on arms and armour, but his activities were not confined to military equipment of former years, for he made careful and exhaustive investigations respecting the costumes, uniforms, manners and customs of later periods. His work under these headings was embodied in articles in journals, technical or popular, and in encyclopaedic works which dealt with the subjects which he had made his life study.'

'For more than twenty-five years he travelled from Ditchley to London to carry out his various duties, and enjoyed to the full the companionship of those whom he met in a third class smoking carriage, saying that he had thereby often obtained information which was very valuable to him in his studies.'

1845
Emile Cartailhac[12] d. 1921

He read law and natural science at the university, but he soon found his real calling as an archaeologist.

'He was attached to the Natural History Museum in Toulouse, in which city he spent the rest of his life, with occasional excursions to attend congresses or to deliver lectures, a form of activity in which he took a keen delight. At the Paris Exhibition of 1867 he was indefatigable, and by means of well-selected series of prehistoric remains and by lectures brought before his countrymen the main facts of prehistoric discoveries. Later he bought from Mortillet the rights of the *Matériaux*,[13] which he edited and managed for twenty years, until it and some other similar publications were merged in the present representative of the subject, *L'Anthropologie*. It is said that his lectures at the Faculty of Science in Toulouse were so popular that the jealousy of his fellow professors was excited, and that by intrigues they succeeded in bringing them to an end. The only result was that it forced Cartailhac more into the literary field and his contributions to scientific periodicals at this time were more numerous than ever.'

'He was essentially an evangelist, ever eager to impart knowledge and with a keen bright mind that inevitably infected his audience.'

Cartailhac was of the Woolley type, an excellent scholar, with a passion for communication and a remarkable ability to stimulate enthusiasm.

1845
Professor Edouard Naville[14] d. 1927

A Swiss, 'he was an imposing figure, a man of great stature, not only physically but in knowledge'.

'One of the last of the older generation of Egyptologists, who did such splendid work in their time for the advancement of Egyptological science, Naville belonged to the generation that followed that of Lepsius, Brich and Brugsch, the three giants who took up the work of the original discoverer, Champollion, and set Egyptology on its feet.'

In Egypt, he worked for the Egypt Exploration Fund. 'When the fund was first started, under the inspiration chiefly of the late Miss Amelia Edwards, he and Mr (now Professor Sir) Flinders Petrie were the two protagonists in the work of excavation begun in the early eighties by that society.'

Many of his finds were brought back to England. 'Naville was always proud to point out in our galleries this statue or pillar or that colossal head that his work had added to our national collections. He liked big things, big trophies; *de minioris non curavit*. The modern insistence on the importance of little things, of small objects of anthropological or artistic value, was incomprehensible to him; and when in later years his assistants insisted on recording a scarab or a few beads with as much care as a colossal statue, he would smile and shrug his shoulders.'

1848
Sir Henry Churchill Maxwell-Lyte[15] d. 1940

Sir Henry was an archivist, who spent forty years reorganising the Public Record Office. From 1886 to 1926 he was Deputy Keeper of the Public Records.

His four chief works, published at long intervals, were his *History of Eton* (1877); *History of Oxford University* (1886); *History of Dunster* (1909); and *Book on the Great Seal* (1926). He was devoted to his ancestral county of Somerset, and until within a few weeks of his death he was at work transcribing the Register of a medieval Bishop of Bath and Wells.

'He was always open to new ideas, and he went by air to Basle on the first stage of his annual holiday when he was 90 years old; but he was in most respects typical of the age to which he belonged. His manner was courteous and dignified; it was unnecessary for him either to praise or blame those who worked under him, as a subtle variation in his manner made it clear whether or not approval was conveyed.'

Sir Henry never soiled his hands or feet in an excavation, but he was a welcome and valued Fellow of the Society of Antiquaries.

1849
Robert de Lasteyrie[16] d. 1921

'M. le Comte Robert de Lasteyrie, Membre de l'Institut and one of our Honorary Fellows', was born in Paris. His grandmother was a sister of Mirabeau. At the university he studied law and archaeology. In 1872 he decided to concentrate on archaeology and the following year became 'archiviste-paléographe'. His eminence in this field led to his appointment as Professor of Medieval Archaeology at the Ecole des Chartes.

'His interests were by no means confined to archaeology. In 1893 he was elected deputy for the Corrèze, the department in which he had his country home, and he was for many years a director of the Chemin-de-Fer de l'Ouest. His fine character commanded the admiration of all who knew him, and was proved by the striking demonstration of respect at his funeral.'

1851
Sir Emery Walker[17] d. 1933

Walker was the head of a firm of process-engravers. He became a Fellow of the Society of Antiquaries in 1902, served several times on its Council and was a Vice-President from 1925 to 1929. In his eighty-first year, he was made an Honorary Fellow of a Cambridge college.

'His lasting claim to remembrance will rest securely on his services to printing. It was fortunate for the future of British typography that he was from 1883 onwards brought into close connection with William Morris in Hammersmith. The foundation of the Kelmscott Press was the direct result of this friendship, and although Walker, for financial reasons, was never formally a partner of Morris in his famous undertaking, he was none the less intimately connected with it and concerned in everything it produced.'

After Morris's death in 1896, Walker joined with T. J. Cobden Sanderson in the starting of a new venture, the Doves Press, carried on at the same high level.

'The improvement in the appearance of the everyday book during the past thirty years or so is almost a commonplace with us, but not everyone is conscious of how greatly the advance is due to the skill and enthusiasm of our late Fellow. No trouble was too great for him to take in this vital matter and his advice was as freely given as it was widely sought.'

'He had a genius for friendship. Few men can have had so many close friends in such widely different stations of life. He found the world a pleasant place because he was pleasant to all the world.'

And of how many of today's scholars and archaeologists could that be truthfully said?

4. *The Right Rev. G. F. Browne, died 1930.*
'*Other archaeologists did not agree with his conclusions, but they were formed after close study and, though often expressed dogmatically, were always provocative of thought and further study.*' (p. 21.)

1851
Dr Panagiotes Kavvadias[18] d. 1929

'Forty years ago, when richer countries were doing little even to protect national monuments, he found means to expand and perfect the Greek archaeological service, and to co-ordinate all available resources, voluntary as well as official, foreign as well as native, for the study and preservation of his country's heritage from the past.'

Born in Cephalonia, he studied archaeology in Munich, Berlin and Paris. In 1877 he became Ephor of Antiquities for the Greek Archaeological Society and from 1881 directed its excavations at Epidaurus.

He was temporarily deprived of his functions during the military revolution of 1909–10, because of his 'virtual dictatorship in archaeological matters', but after two votes of confidence and the dissolution of the Assembly, he was reinstated in his posts in the University and the Archaeological Society and became Chairman of the Archaeological Board, holding his office until 1920.

He was a member of the German Academy of Sciences, a corresponding member of the French Institute and an honorary professor of the University of Leipzig. The Society of Antiquaries elected him an Honorary Fellow in 1893.

'He combined the vision that plans boldly for the future with the tenacity and force of character that enabled him to realise his hopes.'

1855
Lt. Col. George Babington Croft Lyons[19] d. 1926

A regular officer in the Essex Regiment, Col. Lyons devoted much money and effort, especially in the second half of his life, to building up collections of objets d'art, furniture and scientific instruments.

'It is unfortunate that with all his industry in gathering information about the collections he made, Lyons was not one of those who readily sat down to the writing of a note or paper for the Society's publications. Collectors of works of art are too often somewhat indolent in setting down all they know, even about their possessions, and there should be, in every generation, a Farington to gather and record all the fleeting fragments of information that otherwise would disappear for ever.'

'With tastes of this kind and means enough to allow him to indulge them, it was not surprising that Lyons' collections in china, jewellery, prints, furniture, and the minor objects of house decoration, should quickly outgrow the capacity of bachelor chambers in Hertford Street and later of his compact little house in South Kensington.'

'By his will, he bequeathed to the British Museum such of his mathematical instruments as may be desired.'

'He possessed in a high degree that peculiar hospitable gift that attracted to his company men of a type who were eminently agreeable to each other, and whose diverse tastes provided endless food for discussion. In this way many a hare was started that ultimately became a useful prey for the deliberations of the Society, and at Lyons' hospitable board many of us first met men who have since become active Fellows of our body.'

1857
Sir Charles Hercules Read[20] d. 1929

Sir Hercules' career was spent entirely at the British Museum. He became head of the Department of British and Medieval Antiquities at the early age of 39. His connection with the Society of Antiquaries was important both to him and to the Society. He was its Secretary from 1892 to 1908 and its President from 1908 to 1914 and again from 1919 to 1924.

During his sixteen years as Secretary, he was to a large extent responsible for the policy, activities and standards of the Society, 'and his familiarity with antiques, combined with a visual memory that was truly remarkable, made his extempore comments of more than usual interest.'

'As a member of the Society of Dilettanti he found scope for his undoubted artistic perceptions and social inclinations; and, as a lively and agreeable companion, he was cordially welcome in the houses of wealthy collectors.'

1857
Mill Stephenson[21] d. 1937

A Hull man, Stephenson was educated at Richmond Grammar School and at Cambridge. He was called to the Bar in 1885, but never practised.

'Spared from the necessity of having to earn his living, he was able to devote his boundless energy throughout practically the whole of his long life to the pursuit of those antiquarian studies in which he was interested.'

Brass rubbing was one of his hobbies at school and he became an acknowledged authority on monumental brasses. 'It was perhaps his native Yorkshire common sense that made him turn to the more practical side of archaeology and to such tangible objects of antiquity as could be brought within the range of an exact science. In Roman antiquities he was especially interested and acquired a very useful knowledge of them, and in particular of Roman coins, which enabled him to superintend with the utmost efficiency the excavations at Silchester for the greater part of the twenty-odd years during which they were carried out by the Society. Here his remarkable ability to deal with the workmen under him, his ready sympathy with them and understanding of their ways, combined with his strong sense of humour, inspiring their respect and real affection for him, contributed very largely to the harmonious carrying out of the work. In all his undertaking he sought no self-glorification.'

Elected to the Antiquaries in 1888, he served seven times on its Council, and was also Honorary Secretary of the Royal Archaeological Society and of the Surrey Archaeological Society. He ran the Monumental Brass Society until it closed down during the First World War.

The premises of the Society of Antiquaries at Burlington House were his club. 'He was to be found almost any afternoon at his accustomed place in that room of the library which came to be popularly known as 'Mill's parlour.' Here his advice and entirely disinterested assistance were never sought in vain by those whom he knew to be, like himself, genuinely in search of knowledge, although he had a wholesome distrust of those who, he suspected, merely desired to suck his brains for the sake of their own advertisement.'

1857
William Page[22] d. 1934

William Page was trained as a civil engineer, 'but his natural bent for archaeology asserted itself', and at the age of twenty-four he went into partnership with his brother-in-law, W. J. Hardy, to become a professional record searcher and legal antiquary. In 1902 he joined the staff of the *Victoria County History*, sharing the editorship with H. A. Doubleday, and became a sole editor in 1904. It was a good choice.

'His patience and resource, backed with a serene sense of humour, carried him successfully through a long and difficult task, and the troubles and hindrances which the great undertaking experienced were in no sense due to any action of his. On the other hand, it is not too much to say that its successes were almost entirely due to him.'

'Through constrained by the circumstances of his life to be a man of affairs, Page was essentially a scholar and historian; nothing would have been more congenial to him than a learned leisure. The kindliest of men, he was never better pleased than when putting the resources of his great learning at the disposal of his friends, and there are many who are deeply in his debt.'

The remark about 'learned leisure' is significant. Page was born at a time when the scolar could reasonably expect to have a private income sufficent to give him the leisure and independence his work required. Page had to earn his living, but he made the best of the situation.

5. *Somersetshire Archaeological and Natural History Society, Minehead meeting, 1889. Excursion to Porlock.*

1858
Dr Salomon Reinach[23] d. 1933

Born at St Germain, Reinach took a degree at the University of Paris, before becoming a student at the French School in Athens. After this he became Secretary to the Archaeological Commission in Tunis and was then attached to the Museum at St Germain, of which he became Director in 1902.

In 1896 he was elected a Member of the Académie des Inscriptions et Belles Lettres and in the same year he became head of the Museum he undertook the editorship of the *Revue Archéologique*. He became an Honorary FSA in 1907.

'His outlook was truly catholic, and there were few subjects in prehistory, classical or medieval archaeology which he had not studied and on which he had not written. His literary output was enormous. He compiled the official catalogue of the St. Germain Museum before he became its Director; and besides innumerable articles in the *Revue Archéologique* and other archaeological and anthropological periodicals, he had published his well-known *Répertoires* on painting and sculpture, works of religion and myth, on Greek epigraphy, on archaeological field work, and, with M. Bertrand, on the Celts in the Po and Danube Valleys. In his earlier years he had travelled extensively in Greece and the Near East.'

'The Society of Antiquaries highly appreciates the honour of having, for no less than a quarter of a century, so distinguished an Honorary Fellow to represent the home of Prehistory.'

1860
George Clinch[24] d. 1921

After leaving school, Clinch found employment in the British Museum Library and during the nearly twenty years he spent there he wrote several books on the topography of London. He also wrote two papers for the Society of Antiquaries, both of which were published in its *Proceedings*. In 1895 he was appointed Clerk to the Society and in 1910 the Council added the title of Librarian to his office, 'in recognition of his increasing responsibilities and valuable services'. He remained in this post for twenty-five years, retiring the year before he died.

'As an antiquary, he gave special attention to prehistoric archaeology and many of the articles on this subject in the Victoria County Histories were from his pen. As a Kentish man, he was naturally keenly interested in the antiquities of his native county, on which subject he wrote many books and papers, included among them being works on Bromley, Hayes and Keston and the *Little Guide to Kent*, and as a member of the Kent Archaeological

Society he had contributed papers to *Archaeologia Cantiana*. He had also written books on English costume, on old English churches, and on English coast defences. He was a Fellow of the Geological Society and of the Society of Antiquaries of Scotland, and was an active member of the London Survey Committee. In addition, he had served as chairman of the Council of the Association of Men of Kent and Kentish Men.'

'To the Society of Antiquaries during his twenty-five years' service he always showed a great and loyal devotion, and had endeared himself to the Fellows by his ready courtesy and geniality.'

1860
William Paley Baildon[25] d. 1924

Baildon was a lawyer, in full-time practice throughout his working life as a Chancery barrister. Elected FSA in 1892, 'he made frequent communications to the Society, and took a constant part in discussions'. He became Vice-President in 1922 and was holding this office at the time of his death.

'He brought to bear on his archaeological pursuits the careful training of the lawyer; and the precise historical fact which he could often deduce from a medieval document of English character was due to his exact knowledge of medieval law.'

'Genealogy was a branch of knowledge through which the human life of the Middle Ages could be illuminated, and his treatment of genealogy on definitely scientific lines. No pedigree could be accepted which not only did not stand the test of careful scrutiny, but which could not actually be proved in the light of documentary evidence.'

1860
Leland Lewis Duncan[26] d. 1923

Born in Lewisham and educated at a local grammar school, 'he entered the Civil Service as a clerk in the War Office and stayed there, improving his position, until his retirement in 1922.' He was elected FSA in 1890 and received the M.V.O. in 1902, and later an O.B.E.

'Coming under the influence of Challenor Smith, he was led to see how much material of great human interest could be extracted from wills.' Challenor Smith's index of wills and probate at Somerset House was published in 1893 by the British Record Society. Duncan was one of the general editors. 'His interest in wills never waned.'

'He often in his later years regaled his friends with anecdotes of how he used from his earliest days there to slip out of the War Office at luncheon

6. *Somersetshire Archaeological and Natural History Society, Wellington meeting, 1912. The Rev. H. H. Winwood describing the geology of the West Leigh Quarries.*

time and make his way to Somerset House and copy a will or two, and his accounts of the various adventures he had at Somerset House in that connection were very diverting.'

'The Society had a high estimation of his special gifts and took the unusual course of issuing in 1906 an extra volume called *Testamenta Cantiana*, consisting of extracts from various 15th and 16th century wills, giving details of great interest concerning Kentish churches, all those relating to West Kent being contributed by Duncan.'

He was a quite exceedingly friendly man. 'It may be sufficient to recall his modest demeanor, so striking in an antiquary of his attainments, of his ever-ready help to any who might apply to him for assistance in their antiquarian pursuits; and of that lovable disposition which makes his loss so hard to bear by those who were privileged to know him intimately.'

1862
David George Hogarth[27] d. 1927

Educated at Winchester and Magdalen College, Oxford, Hogarth was widely travelled and carried out a considerable number of excavations. In 1908 he became Keeper of the Ashmolean Museum and during the 1914–18 War he was head of the Arab Bureau.

He was elected FSA in 1891 and between 1912 and 1916 he served on the Council as Vice-President.

'The enormous books and reports in which he recorded his travels and the results of his labours as an excavator are marked at once by a breadth of scholarship, considerable literary ability and, above all, a sanity of judgement born of a cool, if anything unenthusiastic vision. Such was the logical outcome of an attitude to archaeology which confessed that in him the antiquarian spirit was not unborn, but was the great accident of his life. The collector's spirit, often the urge of many an excavator and archaeologist, was not essentially his. Beneath his work lay rather the spirit of the skilled traveller, keenly curious of cities and men, not alone for their past, but also for their present and future.'

1862
Lt. Col. William Hawley[28] d. 1941

Hawley was connected with what is referred to as the Society of Antiquaries' second period of field work, the excavations of Old Sarum and Stonehenge. The first period, which lasted from 1888 to 1908, was concerned with the clearing of the site of the Roman town of Silchester. The Old Sarum project became Hawley's responsibility in 1909.

'He was trained in the Royal Engineers, which developed the orderly and accurate habits of mind with which nature had endowed him, and, with many years of experience behind him, he took up his work for the Society with such competence and thoroughness that Old Sarum, in spite of its predominantly medieval aspect, became the meeting place for excavators of all kinds. For those who were privileged to take a share in the work, the wooden excavation hut at Old Sarum will ever be a pleasant memory.

'Hawley was the most modest and self-effacing of men, generous to a fault and greatly appreciative of competence in others, being himself skilled in all manner of ways. From the workshop at his home at Figheldean came a series of neatly made 'gadgets', which he was wont to present to his friends and valued workers; his own excavating tools were as ingenious, neat and clean as their owner. Even the iron bar he used for sounding seemed to have special qualities, so that his colleagues would credit it with the power of distinguishing between a silver and a bronze coin, buried a yard in the ground.'

In 1919, when the Society's activities shifted to Stonehenge, Hawley was also in command and continued operations there until 1926, when about half the area had been excavated.

It is interesting to observe that of the two dozen Fellows of the Society of Antiquaries whose careers have been outlined above, only six had any experience at all of excavation. For those who were members of the various county archaeological societies during the second half of the nineteenth century, the proportion was undoubtedly far lower. So far as the Victorians were concerned, the excavator was simply one of many possible kinds of antiquary, neither higher nor lower in the scale than the rest. The interests of these men, who represented very well what was thought of as archaeology at that time, were remarkably varied – lake dwellings, liturgical texts, metallurgy, wills, genealogy, objets d'art, arms and armour, printing, monumental brasses, medieval churches. The bond between them was a simple one, easily understood – a wish to study some aspect of the past and to make the result of their researches and enthusiasm available to others.

Their occupations covered as wide a range as their interests. One or two had never engaged in any form of gainful employment, possessing that enviable advantage for any scholar, a private income. They were in the position of the retired soldier, whose time was mainly given to the acquisition of beautiful things, and who was charmingly characterised in his obituary as having 'tastes of this kind and means enough to allow him to indulge them'. Others, by their success in their chosen calling, made enough money fairly quickly to allow them to retire early and to practise their hobbies on a full-time basis. Dr Munro can serve as the archetype of this group, a man who toiled for twenty years in his Scottish practice, not unenjoyably, one feels,

7. *Somersetshire Archaeological and Natural History Society, Minehead meeting. Excursion to Dunster Castle, 23rd June 1932.*

until 'his resources were such as to free him from his arduous professional labours'. At that point, 'with his interest steadily fixed on the aspect of the subject which had primarily attracted him, he retired from his practice and devoted himself henceforth entirely to archaeology'.

Those who were unable to arrange their lives as Dr Munro arranged his were counted unfortunate. Fate had not permitted them to fulfil their true destiny. William Page was of this type, and of him one had to say that 'though constrained by the circumstances of his life to be a man of affairs', a euphamism for 'to earn his living', he was 'essentially a scholar and historian; nothing would have been more congenial to him than learned leisure'.

'Learned leisure' was one part, and an important part, of the Victorian dream, and there was and is a great deal to be said for it. The person blessed with it is both a fortunate and a highly developed human type. To be in a state of health and balance, society requires a reasonable proportion of people with the time, money and energy to think. Whether these benefits come as a result of a State grant, a pension, an undemanding job, or a private fortune is immaterial. The Victorian system favoured the private fortune and the undemanding job, but the permutations of the four kinds of leisure-giving support are extremely varied and flexible.

A few of the men in our list might be called professional archaeologists. One was Swiss, another Greek and a third English. The remainder cover the range of middle-class occupations reasonably well: two doctors, three lawyers, a bishop, a printer, a civil engineer, two army officers, two Civil Servants, a librarian, a metallurgist, and three museum people. Three things in particular strike one about both the employed and the unemployed, as human beings. They were enthusiasts, they lived a long time – it was difficult, it seems, for a Victorian archaeologist not to be an octogenarian – and they were kindly, friendly, hospitable people. After making full allowance for the traditional language of obituaries, the appearance over and over again of phrases such as 'lovable disposition', 'happy and hospitable', 'a sense of good fellowship', 'ready courtesy and geniality', 'the kindliest of men', cannot be accidental. These men really did enjoy what they were doing and it was a pleasure for them to share their knowledge and experience with others. The world of scholarship at that time, in archaeology as in other fields, was not the cut-throat, fiercely competitive affair it has become since. Today's archaeologists and academics are, unfortunately, not renowned for their kindness and generosity towards one another. The coming of the Age of the Professional has involved a serious and sad deterioration in human relationships.

It is worth repeating in this connection the two-sentence tribute to Sir Henry Howarth, who symbolises 'learned leisure' at its Victorian best. 'He was of those who, like Bacon, take all knowledge for their province, and so he was often able to suggest analogies between one subject and another which would not occur to the specialist, and it may be that much of the usefulness of his contributions to knowledge is to be traced to this fact. The fact, too, that he had so many interests may also explain the extraordinary freshness of his mind to the end of his eighty-one years.'

With each decade of the twentieth century, the Howarth type of archaeologist became steadily rarer and both archaeology and society are the poorer for it.

2 Rediscovering Britain

It is curious that, without exception, the numerous people who have written about the history of archaeology in Britain should all have ignored the influence of the railways, not only on the growth of a general interest in the past, but on such matters as attendance at meetings and on the organisation and location of excavations. It cannot be an accident that there should have been such a remarkable flowering of local archaeological societies, and of agricultural societies, at the very time when the railway network of Britain had been substantially completed, by the 1860s. For the first time, people could move about the country sufficiently comfortably, cheaply and quickly to make travelling something of a pleasure. It is obvious, and frequently emphasised, that the railways opened up Britain industrially and commercially; what is much less realised, apparently, is the extent to which they had a similar effect on the intellectual life of the nation.

Consider, for example, this extract from the published *Proceedings* of the Society of Antiquaries, relating to some of the Society's regular meetings in 1858.

> The Rev. H. T. Ellacombe, F.S.A., Local Secretary for Devonshire, exhibited drawings of two corbel-heads from the weather-moulding of the west window of the tower of Clyst St. George, near Topsham, in Devonshire. They represented a male head with long wavy moustache and the end of a hood tucked in under the rim of his cap in a very peculiar manner, and the other a female, with a rich head-dress. The date appeared to be about 1470.[1]

In 1858 the Rev. Ellacombe would have probably travelled to London by going to Exeter station by pony and trap, with a servant or one of his family to take the trap home again, and then to Paddington via Taunton by train. He could have left his vicarage after a not-too-early breakfast and been at the Society's premises comfortably by mid-afternoon. He would almost certainly have stayed the night in town, but, had he wished to do so, he could have returned to Exeter overnight on the mail train. The Exeter – London railway link was completed in 1844. Before that, it was a hundred and seventy weary, bumpy miles by coach, necessitating at the very least an extra twenty-four hours and another night in London for the round trip. The Rev. Ellacombe, or any other Devon parson, might well have felt inclined to stay at home, however great his enthusiasm for medieval church architecture might have been. This would have been especially the case during the winter months, when a high proportion of the Society's meetings were held. It was the railway which allowed those members of learned societies living in the provinces to regard travel to London as relatively normal and easy. The change was particularly appreciated by people getting on in years, as many of those who belonged to bodies like the Society of Antiquaries tended to be.

But the railway was an equal blessing to local societies. Before the slaughter of branch lines and the wholesale closure of stations in the 1950s, Britain was wonderfully well provided with railway services and connections, as many people still remember with nostalgia. This splendid network, one of Victorian England's greatest technical and social achievements, gave anyone who had the time and could afford the fare an opportunity to explore their own country to an extent that had never been possible before. The local archaeological societies took full advantage of the possibilities offered and the Excursion became one of the most important features of their pro-gramme. Here are one or two examples of the system.

The first relates to the Suffolk Archaeological Society.

The excursion of this Society has just taken place and a fair number of members and friends found themselves at Needham Market railway station,[2] under the Presidency of Lord John Hervey. Thence they pro-ceeded to Barking Church. From Barking the party returned to Needham Chapel. M. W. Sewell of Yaxley read an interesting paper on its history and antiquities. Creeling St. Mary was the next place on the programme, after which came Stonham Aspal, Mickfield and Stonham Parva. The most important church visited during the day was Earl Stonham. In the new schoolroom at Earl Stonham had been collected a good series of antiquarian remains, obtained in the excavating of a field of about half an acre of glebe.[3]

Needham Market was nicely placed in the middle of the county and from its station there one could travel north, south, east and west with no great difficulty. Members usually made an excursion of this kind a cultural excuse for a little holiday and many of them would reckon to spend three or four days in the area, staying with friends or at a nearby hotel, in this case perhaps at Stowmarket or Ipswich.

The heavy emphasis on churches in the 1871 Suffolk excursion was entirely typical of what was happening over the country as a whole at this time. The Victorians loved churches and could never have enough of them.

8. *General Pitt-Rivers, Britain's first Inspector of Ancient Monuments.*

To a great many people in Britain, churches – that is, Church of England churches – were history in a very prestigious and concentrated form. To be interested in church history and church architecture was to be unassailably correct and respectable and, in any case, a great deal of history of Britain *is* enshrined in its churches and cathedrals. They are our most plentiful and widely distributed museums and, respectability and Godliness apart, it would have been foolish to neglect them. From a Society's point of view, churches had other important advantages. They provided shelter from the rain and wind, a useful asset in the British climate, they contained seats, and in many cases they had a scholarly incumbent who was willing to give the visitors a free and reasonably well-informed talk about the history and notable features of his church. At Earl Stonham, it will have been observed, there was a bonus, since the church glebe contained some kind of archaeological site – we are not told what it was, unfortunately – and a generous selection of objects from it had been laid out for the Society's members to inspect. What they made of the exhibition one can only guess, but it is interesting, and rather sad, to notice that they were not taken to the site. It was the finds they were supposed to be interested in, not the place where they had been found, and in 1871 that was the usual approach.

In the same year, the Sheffield Architectural and Archaeological Society explored their chosen area in a rather more adventurous fashion, with only two churches in the agreeably varied mix. The point of departure was Rotherham.

A party of ladies and gentlemen drove off from the School of Art at about 10 a.m. and on their way called to look at the fine oak room in the Old Hall at Carbrook and the old Roman station at Temple Borough near Rotherham (Ickles), respecting both of which places the Rev. J. Stacey gave some particulars. After visiting Wentworth House (by the kind permission of Lord Fitzwilliam), the party were met at the Church by Mr. Massey, of Wentworth, who pointed out many interesting particulars and read them a capital paper on the ancient history of the place. Returning to Rotherham, the party was met by Mr. J. Guest and Dr. Sherman, who conducted them over the New Hospital, now in course of erection, and after visiting the fine old Parish Church, the party assembled in the Mechanics' Institution to hear Mr. Guest read an interesting paper on the ancient history of Rotherham.[4]

Down in Surrey, however, it was still almost undiluted churches:

The members assembled at Guildford and proceeded by train to Baynards, by the Horsham, and Brighton Railway, where they entered vehicles for the day's drive. The first halt was at Rudgwick Church, in the walls of which are a number of Roman bricks, from some Roman villa destroyed by fire, their appearance fully warranting that conclusion. The Church was described by Mr. W. W. Pocock. The next drive was to Alford, the site of the ancient forest . . .⁵

And so on, to Cranleigh, where 'the party proceeded to a meadow belonging to Mr. Napper, of Cranleigh, where luncheon was served beneath a tent'. Then, in the late afternoon, there was a special train to take them all back to Guildford.

This kind of outing was taking place county by county throughout Britain and, such is the attractiveness of the recipe and the strength of the tradition, it is still going on, although nowadays the members are moved about by coaches and cars, rather than by trains and horse-drawn charabancs. But is was the railways that got the habit established. Two comments are necessary, perhaps. The first is that, since the excursions nearly always took place on a weekday, anyone with a regular job was automatically excluded, although it was easy enough, no doubt, for professional people and those with businesses of their own to take the day off. Consequently it was not the British who were being given the opportunity to learn more about the antiquities of their county or country; it was, with rare exceptions, the upper and upper middle class British. The second point to make is that, although it is easy to criticise the Victorians for their limited choice of places to visit, the fact is that in most areas there were very few historic monuments other than churches which the general public could visit. Prehistoric, Roman or medieval sites where there was anything of consequence to be actually seen were few and far between, the country houses, now the mainstay of the tourist round, were still family homes, where the public was not welcome at all. So, for the most part, it was churches and perhaps cemeteries, or nothing.

It would be fair to say that between the mid-nineteenth century and the 1920s Britain was being rediscovered by the diggers, who were always a small body, and by the above-ground excursionists and antiquarians, who were far more numerous. Sometimes, as at Silchester and Cranborne Chase, the two coincided, where the excavations were sufficiently spectacular and well-organised to justify an expedition for the sake of seeing them, but for the most part the two worlds kept well apart and continued to do so until the better-off members of society began to buy motorcars, which did not happen to any great extent until the early 1920s. Once that happened, the private excursion, undertaken on one's own without the benefit of an archaeological society, became a much more practicable proposition. An hour's visit to a dig in progress became no more than a detour from one's main route through the countryside.

All fashions, however – and archaeology/antiquarianism was a fashion quite as much as it was a hobby or a form of self-improvement – need to have their influential trend-setters, the enthusiasts who have influence and who have the personality and possibly the eccentricity to catch the popular fancy. In the days before broadcasting and mass-circulation newspapers, fashions spread mainly by means of social contacts, and one has to remember that, until the twentieth century, those contacts were extremely local so far as the majority of people were concerned. It was only perhaps ten per cent of the population at most who met at all frequently people from other parts of the country and who read newspapers and periodicals regularly.[6] It may be slightly flattering to describe them as the carriers of ideas, since in many cases all that reading and personal meetings resulted in was a strengthening of existing prejudices, but some of them at least did fulfil that rôle. They were, to use a modern phrase, the opinion formers and, in Victorian England, they exercised that rôle more effectively if they had a title of some kind. A title made their opinion more worth having.

Sir John Evans was in many ways the ideal Victorian opinion-former so far as archaeology was concerned, because he touched life at so many points. Born in 1836, he made a fortunate marriage into the Dickinson family, the Hertfordshire paper-makers and, as a young man, entered the firm as a junior partner. For many years, he did a full day's work in the business and his scholarly activities were pursued entirely in his spare time. He played a full part in the social life of the county and carried out the usual range of public duties which were expected of someone in his position.

He had an early interest in geology and archaeology. In his twenties he excavated a Roman villa at Boxmoor, and he was also interested in coins, as his father had been. Between 1851 and 1872 he published forty-seven papers in the *Numismatic Chronicle*, which he helped to edit. In 1852 he was elected to the Antiquaries, in 1857 he became a Fellow of the Geological Society, and in 1862 a Fellow of the Royal Society.

At the Royal Society, and at the Athenaeum, to which Evans was elected in 1865, he met one of the most interesting and characteristic groups of men whom the age could produce. Neither Academe could claim a share in the enchantment of the Middle Ages; yet, for all their clear paint and shiny varnish, their Turkey carpets and red morocco armchairs, they formed a noble university for a mature mind. There John Evans enjoyed the intellectual comradeship that was his birthright, and became one of a coterie of men, all learned but few trained in academic classicism, who had created sciences out of their own observations and had made in biology, anthropology, palaeontology and archaeology not only new forms of knowledge, but also new ways of thinking about the world and its history.[7]

His great work, *The Coins of the Ancient Britons*, appeared in 1863. Every coin had to be drawn and engraved from originals or castings – reproductions

9. *Excavations at Cranborne Chase at the turn of the century. General Pitt-Rivers' carriage can be seen in the background.*

from photographs were not yet a practical proposition – with the engraver coming down to Evans' home for long periods of work. The book was entirely written after a long day's work either at Nash Mills or at the firm's London office.

John Evans was a regular attender at the meetings of the British Association but, as his grand-daughter recalls, he never really enjoyed them, 'for all the things he cared for were on the margin of its interests.'[8] Although there was nothing in the least amateurish about his own work, he was unhappy at the new trend towards what seemed to him excessive specialisation, with science increasingly divorced from history and broad general culture. So far as he was concerned, an understanding of history was an essential quality of a civilised person and the thought of science outside a context of history repelled him.

How many people may have read or consulted *The Coins of the Ancient Britons*, it is impossible to say. What mattered, however, so far as his influence within the county and within his own class of people throughout Britain was concerned was that a successful, hard-working businessman and pillar of local society should at the same time be a Fellow of the Royal Society and the Society of Antiquaries and that the Universities of Oxford and Dublin should have recognised the quality of his antiquarian studies by awarding him honorary doctorates. The prestige of archaeology among local people who were not scholars of his quality was increased because he so obviously believed that archaeology was important and worthwhile and that educated people should take an informed interest in the past of their own country.

The same could be said of an equally remarkable man, Sir John Lubbock, afterwards Lord Avebury. Born in 1834, he left Eton at the age of fifteen in order to enter the family banking business, which was more to his taste than the studies he was required to pursue at Eton, and thereafter he looked after his own education, with great success.

> He made himself a timetable for the days on which he did not go into the City, mapping out most of his day from 6 a.m. to 12 p.m. The subjects on the timetable included mathematics (which he prepared and took to his father before breakfast), natural history (reading and work with the microscope), poetry, political economy, history, sermons (these he found he could not read later than 10 p.m. without falling asleep) and, finally, German, which kept him awake till midnight.[9]

One begins to understand why he found the classical curriculum at Eton a little restricting. By working out his own plan of attack on the whole field of culture and knowledge, he learnt to concentrate, to sift out the good from the bad, to switch rapidly from one subject to another and, as his biographer puts it, 'to suffer interruption with perfect equanimity'.

Time, he believed, was the most precious of all commodities, to be cherished and saved in every possible way.

No man ever got a greater amount of solid work into his days, or wasted fewer moments. He wore elastic-sided boots – explaining to his family (when they objected) that one could learn a language in the time people took to button or lace up their boots. He always had a book in his pocket for the odd bits of time, and once he was seen correcting the proof of a book in between the acts of a play. Few men ever sat on so large a number of committees and commissions, or belonged to so many societies, for many of which he acted as President.[10]

This was clearly a man whom Victorian England found it easy to respect, the complete Victorian, as Sir Philip Sidney had been the complete Elizabethan, the friend and companion of Charles Darwin, who gave him his first microscope, Fellow of the Society of Antiquaries at the age of 30 and afterwards its President, Vice-President of the Royal Society, Vice-Chancellor of the University of London, President of the Linnaean Society, President of the British Association, President of the London Chamber of Commerce, President of the London University Extension Society, President of the Royal Historical Society, Commander of the Legion of Honour. He wrote books on insects, flowers, fruits and leaves, drawing the illustrations himself, and he was a much-appreciated popular lecturer. 'His sense of humour and a gift for handling weighty subjects not heavily, and for relieving the fatigue of concentration on serious things by an occasional hearty laugh made it a delight to listen to him.'[11]

A strong antiquarian interest ran through his life. At first, he was mainly interested in early graves and tombs in Britain and in dating the implements and ornaments that were found in them. His attention was drawn more and more to the Wiltshire Downs, to their barrows, to Stonehenge and to Silbury Hill. In 1886, he made a careful survey of the Silbury Hill area and, by means of excavation, proved to his complete satisfaction that the Roman road diverged before it reached the Hill and that it had therefore been erected long before the time of the Romans. He was also able to show that the available evidence pointed to Stonehenge being a monument of the Bronze Age, while Avebury was still older.

In 1871, after he had become a Member of Parliament and therefore a person of some political influence, he received an urgent message from the Rector of Avebury, who was well aware of his close interest in the prehistoric stone circles there. The message was to inform Sir John that the site was about to be used for building purposes – this, we should note, was in the 1870s, not the 1970s. The Member for the University of London

10, 11. *Two members of General Pitt-Rivers' staff in the 1880s and 1890s. 10. F. James; 11. Harold St. George Gray. Apart from his archaeological interests, Gray had considerable musical ability. He played the organ regularly and well and had several compositions to his name, including* The Skater's Waltz.

immediately took the most practical step possible. He bought the site himself, which not only saved it for posterity, but gave him the unquestioned right to take Lord Avebury as his title when he received a peerage thirty years later. It was dangers such as this that made him one of the leading crusaders in the growing movement to claim the protection of the State for historic monuments.

The situation was indeed disturbing, and at this point we return to *The Antiquarian*, which had a very good sense of the way in which the wind was blowing in archaeological matters. At almost exactly the moment when the Rector and Sir John Lubbock were getting agitated, with good reason, about the threat to Avebury, the Editor of *The Antiquarian* devoted space in consecutive issues to a thorough examination of the problem, using, it will be noted, the word 'vandalism' to describe what was going on. Under the heading, 'Preservation of Ancient Remains', comes this note:

Referring to a suggestion made by a correspondent of the *Dorset County Chronicle* that clauses against the destruction of stone monuments and similar archaeological landmarks should be inserted in leases, Dr. Christopher Cooke writes to that journal to say that the plan has been adopted by Mr. Forbes, the laird of Culloden in Invernessshire, and doubtless if generally adopted by landlords many old monuments even now might be preserved, which in the absence of such restrictions will cease to be visible before the end of this century.

There seems to be some desire on the part of the Government to assist in such preservation, but not to advance money for the purpose. In Anglesey recently some remains were pointed out to the writer as being those of a comlech which the prior tenant had destroyed in a drunken spree. A fine cromlech at Mathey in Prembrokeshire and another near Marlborough were destroyed by the tenant since the Ordnance Surveys were taken a few years ago. Other instances of vandalism might be recorded.[12]

This is somewhat flattering to landowners, some of whom were undoubtedly as much to blame as the scapegoat tenants, but it was probably sound political tactics to put all the blame on the tenants. What is significant, however, is that by the 1870s the growing national interest in the surviving evidence of Britain's past was producing a concern about the conservation of these monuments. This was something quite new. The earlier part of the Victorian period had shown no interest whatever in safeguarding the relics of the past and certainly no feeling that the Government ought to be doing something about them. When Sir John Lubbock bought Avebury, enough people had become sensitive to the value of history-in-the-field to create a pressure group of sorts, although the size of this should not be exaggerated, and for this the county archaeological societies must certainly be given a

12. *1911. An artist's impression in the* Illustrated London News *of life in Meare Lake Village, Somerset, following the H. St. George Gray excavations there.*

large part of the credit.

The Victorians of the 1870s were the first generation to be seriously faced with the always difficult task of arbitrating between the rival claims of history and tradition on the one hand and progress and a steadily improving standard of living on the other. They had to establish an acceptable balance between their new-found pride in British antiquity and their equally strong anxiety to do nothing that might halt the progress of civilisation. There is no better statement of the dilemma resulting from this problem than the one to be found in *The Antiquarian* two weeks after the remarks about vandalism which have been quoted above. The anonymous writer of this article had his finger accurately and securely on the pulse of his contemporaries as he wrote:

> With the constant increase in population in cities and hamlets and the constant imperative necessity of otherwise occupying the sites of old erections and other artificial human constructions, it becomes quite impossible to many more that our affections would willingly spare. The old and worn – and therefore obscure –must slowly yet inevitably yield to the new and perfect – and therefore plain – as sure as day succeeds to night. The revered footsteps of the past over which gratified generations have worshipfully pondered must gradually become fainter and fainter under the growing traffic of the present.
>
> To mark this absolutism of change over the works of man is both pleasing and profitable, for what is more emotional than to observe the hoarness, the mellowness of the natural final decay, of objects beginning almost from the immemorial. And what is more instructive than the truthful teachings from these crumbling witnesses of human history? We can patiently submit to their slow withdrawal and ultimate disappearance after they have conferred their full delight, knowing that their long-postponed departure is in obedience to a universal law. Such certain loss is impossible to avoid. We can only dutifully support them until their end.
>
> But, while admitting our powerlessness to uphold the manifold monuments of our ancestors, the mute yet eloquent witnesses of their lives and labours, this inability affords no justification or excuse for the wanton removal, alteration or injury of such monuments spared to us by the more compassionate hand of time. The most merciless destroyers everywhere of our historic landmarks are the ignorant and the greedy, who, seeing neither beauty nor utility in these archaic signatures of our forefathers, written here and there on the land, should obliterate them from our gaze and contemplation. Hence the necessity on the part of the antiquarian, the well-informed, to assist individually and unitedly, in arresting needless acts of destruction and damage.[13]

A modern archaeologist or preservationist would probably not put it quite in this way – the Victorians, like modern Americans, found it difficult to be simple and straightforward in public – but the philosophy still holds good today and the situation has not greatly changed. One cannot keep every-thing, the past has to be all the time making way for the present, one should not kill monuments unnecessarily, but support and comfort them to a graceful old age and peaceful death. The enemies of society, whether in the 1870s or the 1970s, are the people whose one aim is to make money, knowing and caring nothing about civilisation or history. The duty of the public-spirited and the enlightened is to be constantly on the watch and to protect the past from those whose concern is wholly and ruthlessly to extract the maximum profit from the present. The Victorians gradually came to realise these sad truths, but they were in no position to effect either a temporary or a final cure for vandalism, which we now see to be a form of chronic social disease.

The first Act to propose any kind of protection for what came to be known officially as ancient monuments was passed in 1882.[14] There were two main reasons why this had not happened earlier. In the first place, there was not a sufficient body of archaeological knowledge and expertise to allow the expenditure of public funds to be justified, no adequate theory on which action could be based. It is significant that Britain's first Inspector of Ancient Monuments, General Pitt-Rivers, was appointed under the provisions of the 1882 Act. Before that there was no way in which the Government could be kept regularly informed and advised as to what the situation actually was and on how it should proceed. Secondly, it was not until the 1880s, when the franchise had been considerably extended, that public opinion had reached a point at which any effective limitations were possible on the rights of private owners to do what they liked with their own property. The series of Ancient Monuments Acts which began in 1882 were a reflection of a growing social conscience which manifested itself throughout the national life and which produced – against stiff diehard opposition, exactly paralleled by that of the landowners who claimed a God-given right to smash up their own cromlechs – unemployment and health insurance, council housing, compulsory educa-tion and regulation of the conditions of employment.

The ancient Monuments Protection Act of 1882 was in no way a great Act, but it was important in being the first occasion on which the State had admitted any responsibility for national monuments or attempted a schedule of outstanding monuments. Nearly seventy monuments in the British Isles were recognised as being of national importance – they included Stonehenge and Avebury – but the protection given even to these by the Act was minimal. It provided that anyone, with the notable exception of the owner himself, who was convicted of damaging or defacing any of the listed monuments would be liable to a fine not exceeding £5 or one month's imprisonment. For £5, in other words, one could have had the satisfaction of

13. *Excavation and re-erection at Stonehenge, 1901–2. Excavating a leaning stone.*

blowing up Stonehenge.

The Act provided secondly that any owner of such a monument should have the power of transferring guardianship of it to the Commissioners of Works, who would then be responsible for its maintenance. In that case, the owner would be treated exactly as a member of the general public if he decided to damage or destroy his own monument. It was a splendidly Gilbertian situation and one wonders very much how the 1882 Act escaped becoming the subject of a Gilbert and Sullivan opera.

There were three further provisions. The Commissioners were empowered, with the consent both of the owner and of the Treasury, to purchase any monument on the schedule, the Commissioners could accept as a gift or bequest any scheduled monument, and, finally, one or more Inspectors could be appointed by the Commissioner of the Treasury, 'to report on the condition of such monuments and on the best mode of preserving the same'. The Act was almost entirely permissive. The Government had no power or obligation to carry out the provisions of the Act, even assuming it wanted to. It was for this reason, more than any other, that General Pitt-Rivers abandoned the job of Inspector after seven years. He was a man who was accustomed to getting things done and, in this case, he realised that nothing was going to be done. The situation remained substantially the same until after the First World War, since the Acts of 1900 and 1910 did very little to lessen the basic weakness of the original Act.

The result was that the preservation or destruction of historic monuments, of whatever kind, depended almost entirely on the interest and goodwill of their owners. There is nothing surprising about this. In an age when private property was sacred, taxation regarded as robbery, and private enterprise considered on all sides to be the prime source of progress, any attempt at regulation or control on the part of the State was bound to meet with suspicion at best and outright hostility at worst. But there was, of course, a positive side to this. If a landowner supported or instigated an archaeological project, that project was very likely to yield useful results, and this not infrequently happened. Silchester and Cranborne Chase were excellent examples of what could happen in an age of completely free enterprise in archaeology. The publicity both received did a great deal to encourage British citizens of all social classes to take an interest in what was being done to discover reliable information about their country's past. They were the two most important archaeological laboratories of the nineteenth century, where every kind of mistake was made and an encouragingly wide range of useful lessons learned.

Silchester belonged to the Duke of Wellington.[15] The site formed part of the estate of Stratfield Saye, which a grateful nation had bestowed on the victor of Waterloo, the conqueror of Napoleon. The old Duke did not have a very high opinion of antiquaries and is reputed to have said to one of them, when the subject of Silchester was raised, that 'he had better go to Rome, where he might find much finer remains'. His successors, however, took a different view. The second Duke was responsible for excavations being started at Silchester in 1864 and the third, in 1890, agreed to the request of the Society of Antiquaries to carry out a complete excavation of the walled town.

The local Rector, the Rev. J. G. Joyce, was appointed to supervise the first dig. Born in 1819, he was the son of a merchant of Clonmel, County Tipperary. He went up to Oxford late, at the age of twenty-four, and after graduating in 1846 he proceeded to take Holy Orders. He became Rector of Stratfield Saye in 1855 and he was the second Duke of Wellington's personal choice for the direction of the excavations at Silchester. He was elected a Fellow of the Society of Antiquaries after three seasons' work on the site, where he had only four labourers to help him. The second Duke provided support and encouragement, but very little money. Joyce had a natural talent for archaeology. As his journal and sketchbook[16] show, he was methodical and understood the need for careful recording. There is good reason to believe that he was the first person to understand the basic archaeological principle of dating structures by means of objects discovered during the excavation, an important step forward for which he has never been given sufficient credit, prestige being reserved in the matter for the later, but much better connected, wealthy and publicity-minded General Pitt-Rivers. The Society of Antiquaries, however, was in no doubt about his ability, as its obituary of him makes clear. 'As an artist and an archaeologist, Mr. Joyce exhibited powers of a high order. No one can be surprised that in early life he was urged to make art his profession.' A sensitive, creative man, he had a real feeling for the past and an excavation, for him, was essentially a way of developing a better awareness of the life and attitudes of the people who had built and lived in what he was now, after the lapse of many centuries, uncovering to view. It is not easy to say the same of most Victorian archaeologists.

Joyce was very much a working parson. The Silchester excavation was merely an addition to his duties. He was kept extremely busy on parochial affairs, largely because of the poverty and distress which was general in the district at the time, and it is quite possible that this constant awareness of human problems made him a better archaeologist, in that it never allowed him to forget that life, and therefore history, is essentially about people, not objects. He had limited means and until 1877, the year before his early death at the age of fifty-nine, he was never able to afford a curate.

After Joyce had gone, the Silchester project dragged on lamely until the death of the Duke in 1884 put a stop to it for the time being. By 1889, however, the Society of Antiquaries and a number of influential supporters were beginning to plan something much more ambitious, a complete

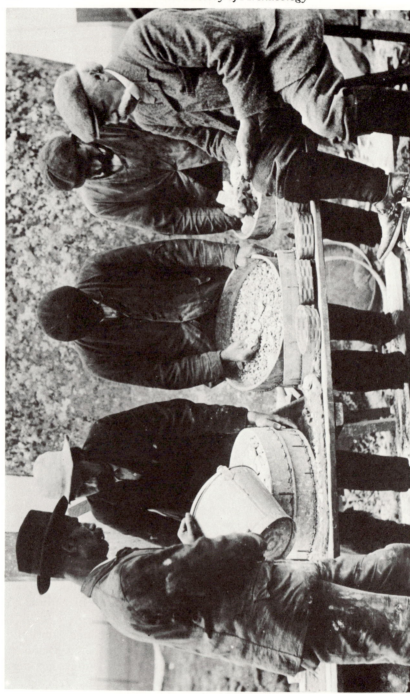

14. *Stonehenge, 1901–2, sifting excavated soil.*

excavation of the 140-acre site. Pitt-Rivers was deputed to sound out the new Duke and discover his wishes in the matter. A letter from him to the Duke has survived and illustrates admirably the way in which archaeological work in Britain was completely dependent on the goodwill of whoever owned the site in question, and the degree of deference which was needed in order to reach the desired end.

The letter, dated 25 June 1889, reads:

General Pitt-Rivers presents his compliments to the Duke of Wellington and writes to say that he called this morning in his capacity of government inspector of ancient monuments to enquire his views and wishes as to the excavation of Silchester. The Antiquaries are very anxious that it should be thoroughly dug out and afterwards covered in again, after plans and a model have been made of it. Being a monument of great national interest, it appears desirable that it should be done. But General Rivers did not wish to take part in any agitation of the accomplishment of such a purpose without first ascertaining the Duke's wishes on the subject. No doubt, if the place were thoroughly explored, after proper compensation to the tenant, it were best in this climate to cover it over again, as it could not be put under cover without great expense. The matter would be thus concluded and there would be no further desire to meddle with the land.

Silchester, it should be noted, was not a scheduled monument under the Act of 1882, so the Duke or his tenant would have been perfectly at liberty to build a cowhouse on the site or turn it into an ornamental lake, had their inclinations gone in this direction. Too much attention should not be given to Pitt-Rivers' reference to having the place 'thoroughly dug out', although this might, to a modern archaeologist, suggest clumsy, unscientific methods of work. What matter is the tone of the letter. Her Majesty's Inspector of Ancient Monuments was perfectly familiar with the etiquette and tactics required on such an occasion, and his approach was completely successful. The Duke approved the scheme, offered a site for a museum to house the finds, a contribution towards its cost and assistance with roofing over any remains thought worthy of being kept open.

The Society of Antiquaries then moved in what would nowadays be called project managers. The excavation was put in charge of George E. Fox, 'artist, architect and student of Roman Britain', and W. H. St John Hope, a medievalist and a senior official of the Society. When work started in 1884, Fox was 51 and Hope, 30.

The financial arrangements for what was much the biggest and best organised excavation to have taken place in Britain up to that time were interesting. An Excavation fund was set up, supported by the Society itself as well as by public subscription. The wage bill varied between £250 and £500 a year, the only other single item of any consequence being the tenant's compensation for his land, about £40 a year. The labourers came from villages within a radius of about six miles. They had to be at work by six in the morning and they were paid half-a-crown a day. If they were required to carry out any particularly dirty work, such as clearing out puts and wells, they received an extra payment. For every coin they came across, they had a halfpenny and for any piece of stonework with a carved inscription on it 3d a letter. The men who discovered a hoard of silver coins in 1894 found themselves better off by a sovereign each.

Some of the labourers were allowed and perhaps encouraged to act as guides to the large numbers of visitors who came to look at the excavations on Sundays, travelling to either Mortimer or Bramley Station by train and then by trap to the site. On a fine Sunday, the people who owned the traps reckoned to do excellent business, and there is no doubt, too, that the labourers supplemented their wages to an appreciable extent in this way. It is probable, too, that quite a number of coins and other items discovered in the course of the excavations found their way illegally into private hands, since the visitors were prepared to pay a good deal more than the Society of Antiquaries' official rate for them.

Silchester certainly gained from its proximity to Reading,[17] and the Great Western main line, which made it a comparatively simple matter for Londoners and for people who lived in large parts of Hampshire, Berkshire and Oxfordshire to plan a day's outing to the site. For many people in the South of England, it was Silchester that showed them what archaeology was all about and what its possibilities and importance were.

As a public relations exercise, the excavations carried out by General Pitt-Rivers on his estate at Cranborne Chase in Dorset proceeded rather differently, mainly as a result of the strongly authoritarian temperament of the General himself. He was born in 1827 into an aristocratic, landed family in Yorkshire. After Eton and Sandhurst, he entered the Army and served in it for twenty-two years. He was elected FSA in 1863 and FRS in 1876. Charles Darwin was one of his sponsors for the Royal Society and he was recommended as being 'distinguished for his original researches in the development of Implements and Weapons and the origins of arts throughout the world, and eminent as a general Ethnologist and Archaeologist'.

In 1880 he inherited the Cranborne Chase estate from his uncle, Baron Rivers, and devoted himself to exploring the antiquities of his own estate. He was, incidentally, a diabetic, and in pre-insulin days, this imposed certain limitations on his energy and activities. All the excavation at Cranborne Chase was done by farm labourers, supervised by a small team of assistants, who, for some strange reason, were known as 'clerks'. The highest paid clerk received £150 a year and probably lived out, but the remainder got much less. Harold St George Gray,[18] who began work on the site in 1888 when he was

15. *The Stonehenge Committee, 1901–2. The two gentlemen on the extreme left and the one on the far right have not been identified, but the others, from left to right, are: E. R. Doran-Webb; C. H. Ponting; Col. Sir Edmond Antrobus; Lord Dillon; Bishop G. F. Browne; Sir Hercules Read; Dr Gowland; Sir William H. St. John Hope; Lady Antrobus; and N. N. Storey-Maskelyne.*

16. *Excavation at the Sanctuary, Wiltshire, June 1930. The owner of the legs is probably W. E. V. (Willy) Young, the site foreman.*

sixteen and remained there for eleven years, had to make do with £24 a year to begin with and was eventually thought to be worth the not exactly generous figure of £65. One has to remember, however, that Gray, like most of the assistants, lived in at the museum, so that the value of his board and lodging has to be added to his salary. They had no professional qualifications, no career structure and no security. Any increase in their salaries was entirely at the whim and discretion of the General.

For less than £600 Pitt-Rivers was able to employ three assistants full-time and fifteen labourers for six months. By the standards of today, this was very much archaeology on the cheap or, as some might be inclined to put it, gross exploitation. It is only fair to point out, however, that no comparable training was available anywhere else in Britain and that to have worked with General Pitt-Rivers was a recommendation second to none. He was certainly a martinet, and on occasions not the most pleasant of people. One did not argue with him and one either accepted his methods of working or one left as quickly as possible.

His character showed itself in what might be called his educational work. Believing very firmly that museums were good for people, but also that there was no harm in combining learning with well-planned relaxation, he established both a museum and pleasure grounds on his estates. In 1900, 44,000 people went there to picnic, listen to the band and look at museum exhibits. His own tenants and workers and their families were obliged to pay regular visits to the amenities provided for them at Cranborne Chase but, even allowing for this, the numbers who came were remarkable. It demanded considerable effort; one took a train and then went a couple of miles on foot. The collections and displays covered both ethnographical and archaeological material and they were arranged entirely by type and category, with no attempt at all to present them attractively, or indeed to explain them. To anyone not blessed with the General's filing-cabinet kind of mind, the rows and rows of objects, tightly packed together, must have seemed utterly bewildering. The great man had no taste or gift for communication or popularisation. Like many other Victorians, he had a distinctly Calvinistic view of knowledge and self-improvement. Learning should not be made too easy.

What he was trying to accomplish as an archaeologist is clearly set out in a paragraph of his monumental account of the excavations he carried out at Cranborne Chase over so many years.

> Tedious as it may appear to some, to dwell on the discovery of odds and ends, that have, no doubt, been thrown away by their owners as rubbish, and to refer to drawings, often repeated, of the same kind of common objects, yet it is by the study of such trivial details that Archaeology is mainly dependent for determining the dates of earthworks; because the chances of finding objects of rarity in the body of a rampart is very remote. The value of relics, viewed as evidence, may on this account be in an inverse ratio to their intrinsic value.[19]

The last sentence is possibly the most important ever written by any archaeologist of any period, but what it implies is unlikely to make the pulse of the general public beat faster. There is no poetry, no romance, no excitement of the treasure-hunt in it, simply the plain statement of scientific fact. Pitt-Rivers had absolutely no gift for dramatising archaeology and no wish to do so, yet he possessed a powerful charisma which drew people to him and made anything with which he was associated seem important and worthwhile. Nobody except those who depended on him for a livelihood, was forced to go to his strait-laced museum and well-disciplined pleasure-grounds, yet each year tens of thousands did and came back for more. To a great extent, this must have been due to the personality and reputation of Pitt-Rivers himself, the impresario who scorned the rôle but enjoyed the power. Without such a stimulus, it was only the discovery of remarkable or valuable things – jewellery, gold, silver, mass graves, foundations of a palace, splendid Roman pavements – which were likely to catch the attention of the

17. *Roman Britain revealed. Excitement around a Roman pavement unearthed in London, 1869, as shown by the Illustrated London News.*

newspapers and in this way to arouse public interest. However important a particular site or particular finds on it might be scientifically – and most archaeology in Britain has tended to be of this kind – some extra element of drama, legend, myth or disaster had somehow to be associated with it if it were to attract the attention of more than a few specialists. Battles, massacres, Romans, Vikings, Druids and saints were always useful in this respect, even if excavation and the careful interpretation of the results should happen to make nonsense of the legends, which was not infrequently the case. In fact – and this is one of the great ironies of both history and education – a century of painstaking, scientific archaeology has done remarkably little to change popular beliefs about our national past. Ideas about Boadicea, Romans, Saxons and those remarkable people commonly known as Ancient Britons are very little different now from what they were in the time of our great-great-grandparents. Archaeology and the vast publicity given to it by television may have made millions of people more interested in history in a vague and general way, but they have left the fairy-tales about our ancestors and our folk heroes largely intact. It may be, as Sir Mortimer Wheeler has suggested, that every country needs two kinds of history, fact, to satisfy the scholars, and fiction and myth, to keep the rank and file of humanity interested and in good heart.

Or, as the proverb so rightly and wisely says, you can lead a horse to the water, but you cannot make him drink. There is a famous passage in Sir Arthur Evans' inaugural address, delivered in 1884 as Keeper of the Ashmolean Museum in Oxford which unconsciously makes the point brilliantly well. Sir Arthur began:

> Consider for a moment the services rendered within quite recent years by what has been called Prae-historic archaeology, but which in truth was never more Historic, in widening the horizon of our Past. It has drawn aside the curtain and revealed the dawn. It has dispelled like the unsubstantial phantoms of a dream those preconceived notions as to the origins of human arts and institutions at which Epicurus and Lucretus already laughed, before the days of biblical chronology. It has taught us that, at a time when Britain formed still a part of the Continent of Europe, with an arctic climate and another fauna; when the Thames was flowing into the Rhine, and the Rhine itself, perchance, was a tributary of 'that ancient river', the river Solent, when the very valley in which Oxford stands was only partly excavated, Man was already in existence here fashioning his flint weapons to aid him in his struggle against the sabre-tooth Tiger or the woolly-haired Rhinoceros.[20]

It may be so, but of whom was Sir Arthur thinking when he spoke of the services performed by archaeology in 'widening the horizon of our Past' and in 'drawing aside the curtains and revealing the dawn'? To what proportion of his fellow-countrymen did he imagine this dispelling of ignorance and half-truths referred? It is extremely doubtful if he ever considered the matter in these terms at all, but, in equating himself and other scholars and educated people with the nation as a whole, he was displaying a curious lack of insight and perspective. When anyone uses the words, 'we', 'us' and 'our', it is always useful and necessary to ask who is meant. And the answer is not infrequently unwelcome.

3 The Influence of the Middle Eastern Spectaculars

During the eighteenth and much of the nineteenth centuries, the archaeology of Britain had something of a second-best flavour about it. 'It was not everyone,' as Glyn Daniel has pointed out, 'who could afford to travel widely in classical lands, and, for such, the study of British antiquities provided a cheap and interesting substitute near at hand.'[1] Professor Daniel goes on to say:

> The literary movement known as the Romantic Revolt clothed in attractive garments the British substitute for classical archaeology. Scholars turned away from the classical light to barbaric gloom and romanticised the Ancient Britains and the Druids, and the local British antiquities attributed to them. The study of the picturesque in the landscape promoted an interest in those obvious picturesque and romantic features – the ancient barrows, forts, standing stones and hut circles – about which written history said so little. And what could be more romantic and exciting than the excavation of these strange antiquities?[2]

This is undoubtedly true so far as its basic premise is concerned – there was a British substitute for classical archaeology – but, according to one's point of view, it either flatters or underestimates the classical archaeologists. Is it really possible that these men, whether one labels them scholars, travellers or collectors, could visit strange countries, hear strange languages, see remarkable landscapes, buildings and ruins and encounter exotic customs without any emotional response at all? How helpful is it to follow the traditional distinction between the ice-cold, wholly objective scholar, a man largely composed of head and brain, and the warm, emotional romantic, a man who is wholly heart and passion? The first is a monster and the second a scatter-brained nuisance. Neither is credible as a human being, although there may well be considerable advantage in both cases in presenting a grossly oversimplified version of oneself to the public. It was, so to speak, good for business. The social historian, however, is under no obligation to believe the fiction and rôle-playing which have been offered to him. He may well decide that, although they may have chosen to pretend otherwise, the men who travelled and sometimes dug in Mesopotamia, Egypt and Greece were just as much romantics at heart as the parson and country gentlemen who stayed at home to weave fantasies around megaliths and barrows. One is entitled, in any case, to have a rather low opinion of anyone who could stand on the site of Carthage or in front of the ruins at Baalbek without dreaming of these places as they had been in their heyday. If the scholar has necessarily to be regarded as the antithesis of the poet, then our culture is indeed in a bad way.

But what evidence is there that our ancestors did in fact regard themselves in this bizarre fashion? It is ourselves, generations later, who have decided to remodel and distort their attitudes to suit our own convenience. The scientists and the poet-romantics have both tried to trace their pedigrees a decent distance backwards and to discover friends and allies in the past. This has certainly been good for their own morale, but it has not made the interpretation of history any easier. 'Inside every fat man,' wrote W. H. Auden, 'is a thin man trying to get out'. One could usefully paraphrase this by saying that inside every scientist and scholar there is a poet trying to get out. Some wilfully and to their own disadvantage deny this, others are glad of the opportunity and encouragement to admit it.

There is no harm in having such thoughts in one's mind as one examines the developing pattern of Mediterranean and Middle Eastern archaeology during the past two hundred years. Between 1750 and 1830 a series of English travellers and collectors were visiting Greece, Syria, Palestine, and Egypt, drawing, measuring, digging, acquiring and, one is permitted to believe, marvelling and brooding. They brought back with them both ideas and, to use a blunt term, loot. They stole and purchased for trifling sums large quantities of items which formed part of the heritage of the countries they robbed in the name of science and scholarship, and with very rare exceptions this material has never been returned to its rightful owners. The museums of North-West Europe and America are crammed with it, as they are with the cultural heritage of Africa, South America and the Pacific. It is dishonest to pretend otherwise, however much one may justify and dignify the process by saying that the discovery and importation of these objects opened the eyes of Europeans and Americans to the achievements of civilisations other than their own and in this way broadened their sympathies and increased their respect for parts of the world which they might otherwise have continued to regard as benighted and backward.

What actually happened was that the scholar-pirates went where the political, military and naval power of their own countries made it safe and profitable for them to go. Because Britain, France and, later, Germany were powerful countries in the nineteenth and early twentieth centuries, travellers, collectors and archaeologists of these nationalities were able to feel relatively secure in moving about, in pursuing their investigations, scholarly or otherwise, and in bringing back more or less what they could get away with, although, as we shall see, there were occasionally certain local difficulties about this.

For a short time, the French were given exceptional advantages, as the result of the successful military operations of that arch-romantic, Napoleon Bonaparte, for whom it was entirely in character to harangue and invigorate his troops with sentences like: 'Soldiers! Forty centuries look down upon you from the top of the Pyramids!' Napoleon's expedition, which arrived in Egypt in 1798, was accompanied by a team of experts specially selected to investigate, survey and record the antiquities of the area. The French Egyptian Institute was set up in Cairo and a number of choice items, including the Rosetta Stone, removed to France as quickly as possible. When British naval and military successes made it necessary for the French to leave Egypt in a hurry in 1801, the British, thinking, as always, only of scholarship, took óver the major part of the Napoleonic collections of Egyptian material and shipped them back to England. In due course, these found their way to the British Museum, where, of course, they still are, and not to the Louvre, which is what Napoleon had in mind.

Merely to put later developments into their proper historical perspective, the notable contribution of French archaeologists and historians in the Middle East needs to be emphasised. Among them was Mariette, sent out to Egypt in 1850 by the Louvre to look for Coptic manuscripts, and who soon went beyond his original brief. He excavated the Serapeum at Memphis and stayed on to become the first Director of the newly established Egyptian Service of Antiquities, largely as a result of the political machinations of Ferdinand de Lesseps and Napoleon III. During the twenty years he spent in this post, he carried out an extensive programme of excavation, on sites which included the Temple of the Sphinx at Gizeh and the cemeteries at Sakkarah. As an archaeologist, he certainly had his faults. He was obsessed with the grand and was chiefly interested in getting newsworthy results, which meant above all valuable and impressive finds. To achieve this, he practised ruthless methods, including the use of dynamite. The everyday objects of the past meant little to him, and any thought of conserving sites and of keeping in mind the needs of later scholars was foreign to him. The recording and publication of his work was most inadequate; his aim as an archaeologist was to build up as large a collection as possible of the objects that interested him.

His great achievement – and it was an important one – was to set up an organisation to keep Egyptian antiquities in Egypt and to establish at least the foundations of an Egyptian National Museum. As part of his campaign on both these fronts, he insisted on having a monopoly of the excavations carried out in Egypt. For many years, he was the sole excavator, a state of affairs which caused other archaeologists with an interest in the Middle East to turn their attentions to countries where more liberal conditions prevailed.

18. *1877. The* Illustrated London News *sends its artist to Mycenae. Schliemann's discoveries at Mycenae stir the British imagination. Rock-cut chamber in the treasury of Atreus.*

Among these areas was Mesopotamia, where field archaeology had been begun a long time previously by the British Resident in Baghdad, Claudius James Rich. Rich's official duties were not onerous and left him plenty of time for the exploration of the sites of ancient cities in Mesopotamia and for building up an extensive collection of manuscripts and antiquities. Rich attempted no excavations, but the account he published of his travels[3] produced considerable interest abroad, especially in France. Paul-Emile Botta, the French consul at Mosul, was responsible for the first excavations in Mesopotamia, at Nineveh in 1842 and at Khorsabad in 1843, which he paid for himself. His discoveries persuaded the French Government to produce funds to allow the work to continue and to be properly published. Five handsome volumes of drawings and text appeared in 1849–50, many of the Khorsabad sculptures discovered by Botta having already been trans-ported to Paris, where they are on display in the Louvre. The French Government continued to take an active interest in the work in Mesopotamia and after Botta's return to Paris Victor Place was appointed to succeed him, with funds to carry on with the excavations at the great Assyrian palace at Khorsabad.

19. *Interior of the treasury of Atreus.*

A little later than Botta, the British archaeologist, Sir Henry Layard, had begun operations at Nimrud, the Biblical city of Calah. He worked there from 1845 until 1847, at first financing the work from his own pocket and from the generosity of the British Ambassador to Turkey, Stratford Canning, and later from a subsidy provided by the British Museum. Despite the fact that it made a very good thing out of the investment – the material shipped back by Layard occupies an important place among its collections – the Museum failed to persuade the British Government to pay for the publication of Layard's work in the way the French Government had done for Botta. Layard was able, however, to find some consolation in the fact that his book, *Nineveh and Its Remains*, sold 8,000 copies in its first year, 'which will,' he wrote afterwards, 'place it side by side with *Mrs. Rundell's Cookery.*'[4] A shortened version of this, *Nineveh and its Remains*, published in 1851, did even better. It was intended primarily for the bookstalls on railway stations and it is entitled to the honour of being the first genuinely popular book on archaeology ever written.

In Layard's day, and for long afterwards, English people of all classes were in a good position to receive news of discoveries in Mesopotamia, Palestine and Egypt. They had a thorough knowledge of the Bible and the people and places mentioned in it were familiar to them as a result of generations of church-going, sermon-listening, and Bible reading. The Bible lands were real in a way that the territory and cultures of classical Greece and Rome were not. With places like Nineveh and Jerusalem and Babylon, and people like Nebuchanezzar they were among friends.

The Victorians did not neglect the other Biblical regions of Palestine and Syria. The Palestine Exploration Fund was established in 1865 and five years later it began a series of surveys and excavations. Sites in and around Jerusalem were excavated in 1867–70 and later, in 1891–92, Flinders Petrie was at work for the Fund at Tell el-Hesy.

Petrie had the great good fortune to have been born at the right time, and of the right stock. His mother was the daughter of Captain Matthew Flinders, R.N., the Australian explorer, and he was twenty-seven and beginning his archaeological career when Mariette's dictatorial reign as Director of Archaeology in Egypt came to an end. Mariette's successor, Sir Gaston Maspero, was a more tolerant man, who saw the value of allowing other countries besides France to take a share in the huge and costly task of excavating sites in Egypt. The National Museum in Cairo, however, kept the right to acquire any antiquities acquired in the course of excavations, although it did on occasions permit the export of objects of relatively minor importance.

Archaeologists are not celebrated for their generosity, but there is common agreement that Petrie was one of the few geniuses that subject can boast. His very long life – he was born in 1853 and he died, fittingly in Jerusalem, in 1942 – covers virtually the whole period in which archaeology as we understand it today was created; and he was personally involved in many of its more significant changes. No excuse is therefore required for devoting a page or two to him, since he summarises and embodies so much of the context within which archaeology operated in the course of what one would think of for other people as two very full working lives.

The Egypt Exploration Fund, which later acquired the rather more active and permanent sounding name of the Egypt Exploration Society, was established in 1883[5] and W. M. Flinders Petrie, as he then was, was appointed its director in the field. His close collaborator, Margaret Murray, who lived even longer than he did, had much to say about him when she looked back on her life on the occasion of her hundredth birthday. She admired him immensely, not only for what he did, but for the kind of giant he was. He began with no advantages apart from a remarkable intelligence, a superb constitution, extraordinary energy and a fine presence, a combination of gifts which proved fully adequate to overcome his lack of social contacts and formal education. Petrie rose to fame, as Margaret Murray justly emphasises, 'without the training of school or university, a condition which in those days was regarded as almost without education. He knew little Latin and less Greek, yet he had a profound knowledge, obtained from good translations, of all the information about Egypt recorded in ancient authors.'[6]

The Secretary of the Egypt Exploration Fund was Miss Amelia B. Edwards, a well-known popular novelist of the day. Following a visit to Egypt, she became extremely interested in both Egypt and archaeology and decided to apply part of her not inconsiderable earnings to this field of scholarship. She eventually founded the Edwards Chair of Egyptology at University College, London, and in 1893, two years after her death, Flinders Petrie became the first Edwards Professor there.

When he took up his post with the Exploration Fund in 1883, Petrie wrote to Miss Edwards in terms which made it clear that the prospect excited him. 'The prospect of excavating in Egypt', he told her, 'is a most fascinating one to me, and I hope the results may justify my undertaking such a work.' Neither of them was disappointed. He worked there every season for many years, returning in between to London to write up his results for publication, to give lectures and to arrange exhibitions. There was also the matter of his Professorship. It was regarded as a part-time arrangement and his salary was one hundred pounds a year. Out of this he had to pay, from his own pocket, twenty pounds a year to a Mr Griffith for the classes in the interpretation of hieroglyphs. After a while Mr Griffith resigned, and the work was divided. Margaret Murray fills in the practical details for us. She recalls:

> Dr. Walker took on the advanced class and I took the elementary class. Dr. Walker, being comfortably off, refused any salary. I accepted the money and used it entirely for out-of-pocket expenses in regard to my training. But I had no qualification whatever for the post. I had never passed an examination in my life. I had never been to school, I had never been to college. My work at University College was my only qualification and the recommendation depended entirely upon Professor Petrie's word.[7]

As Professor Daniel has lamented, 'there have not been enough autobiographies of archaeologists',[8] so one should be especially grateful for one which is as charming and forthright as Dr Margaret Murray's. Born and mostly brought up in Calcutta, where her father was in business, she received her formal education from a governess and at the age of twenty entered Calcutta General Hospital as a 'Lady Probationer Nurse', her father having permitted her to do this for three months and not a day longer.

In 1893, she was in Madras with her sister Mary, who had just had her first baby, and her future career came over the horizon in the most unexpected way. Mary was reading the weekly edition of *The Times*:

> when suddenly she said in an excited voice, 'Oh, it says here that Flinders Petrie is going to hold classes for Egyptian hieroglyphs in London at

20. *The great populariser of the 1920s. Sir Leonard Woolley and his foreman, Hamoudi, in the porch of the expedition house.*

University College'. 'And who is Flinders Petrie?' I asked, never having heard the name before. Then Mary was really angry at my appalling ignorance and want of interest. When her wrath had subsided, she said, 'Now that I am married I can't go to these classes myself, but you must. So you will write at once to Dr. Petrie and say you wish to attend his classes, and I will write to Mama and tell her that she too must write to him and say that you will attend the classes.' Mama and I always did what Mary told us to do and that is how I came to Egyptology.[9]

By the turn of the century Petrie had accomplished what he had set out to do in Egypt, which was to use the archaeological evidence to get Egyptian history into its right order, so that later investigators could fit their discoveries into the correct chronological place. He introduced new methods into archaeological work, making it a suitable university subject. One of his most important achievements was to make archaeologists, and the people who supported them financially, aware of the significance of small and apparently uninteresting objects. His book, *Historical Scarabs*, was a good example of this. In it, he pointed out the scientific value of this kind of material, which had previously been either thrown away or, if it were thought pretty enough, set in a modern brooch or bracelet. Petrie, in fact, systematised archaeology and turned it from a hobby into an organised study, with consequences, some good and some bad, that we shall discuss later.

His methods on the site sometimes annoyed other archaeologists. He took great care of the men he employed and even minor accidents among them were rare. They were always paid the full market price for anything they found, so that they should never be under any temptation to engage in private negotiations with dealers. If, however, anyone did happen to be convicted of this supreme crime, he was dismissed immediately, no matter how good or experienced he might be.[10] No mechanical transport of any kind was used on the site; everything was carried to the dump in baskets. This was laborious and, at first sight, expensive, but it proved, in fact, to be sound practice. Each time a basket was emptied, there were eagle eyes watching to see if there was anything of value in the load. Nothing was missed.

Petrie, unlike some of his colleagues, held strong views about what should and should not be done with the money that had been subscribed for the excavation fund. It was certainly not to be frittered away on luxurious living for the director and his staff. They lived in mud-brick huts and conditions were simple in the extreme.

Every year a supply of groceries and tinned food was sent out from London to the camp in large wooden packing cases. Each case held a carefully calculated supply for a certain number of people for a week. These cases, full or empty, were the furniture. One at the head and one at the foot supported a wire-wove mattress and its frame; a thin mattress, pillows, blankets, sheets and pillow-cases were the bedding. An up-ended case with a tin or enamelled basin and a tooth-glass formed the washstand. A small narrow packing-case, also up-ended, stood by the bed-head and held a flat candlestick with candle and matches. At the end of the season these empty wooden cases were used for packing the finds.[11]

And, in deference to the religious feelings of his workmen, who were, of course, Moslems, Flinders Petrie permitted no alcohol or pig-meat in any form in the camp. There was no bacon and no sausages, which some of his assistants, with pleasant memories of Victorian breakfasts, found a little hard to bear.

Petrie really was a man of whom it could be said that his work was his life. A scholar and of very simple tastes, all he asked were the means and conditions which allowed him to work. He was scrupulously honest and direct, took no pleasure in political intrigues and for the most part managed to keep clear of them, but other eminent British archaeologists who were active in the Middle and Near East revelled in this aspect of the work, sometimes all too obviously, and not infrequently contrived to live in considerable style while directing operations on the site. Sir Arthur Evans, the hero of Knossos, was one of them. Growing up in the shadow of his famous archaeologist father, Sir John Evans, may have been in some ways a difficult experience, but it had its compensations, among them being an abundance of social and professional contacts, a comfortable home, an allowance of £250 a year and a father who could always be relied on to help one out in a financial emergency. Partly, no doubt, because of these advantages, his career moved fast.

After successful educational years at Harrow and Oxford, he travelled extensively in the Balkans during the early 1870s and wrote articles for the *Manchester Guardian* about the explosive political situation there. The Turks still controlled much of the area, but revolutions and independence were in the air and the young Evans enjoyed himself, taking a little time off to marry the daughter of the well-known historian, E. A. Freeman. In 1884 he was elected Keeper of the Ashmolean, at a time when the University of Oxford had begun to realise the value of classical archaeology and was about to appoint a professor in the subject. For the next few years, it took a lot of his time to persuade the University to put the Museum on a proper footing, but by 1891 he had done as much as he felt he could do in this direction and his thoughts were turning towards Crete, where the archaeological problems were exceedingly complex and where there was obviously a reputation to be made.

Great cunning, patience and diplomatic skill were required – Evans had all three in full measure – in order to buy or control the site, at a time when

21. *The blood and slaughter of archaeology. The* Illustrated London News *dramatises Woolley's discoveries at Ur, 1923. Fifty-nine people – men and women – along with six oxen, sacrificed at a Sumerian king's burial: the 'shambles' beside the tomb (broken diagrammatically to show the interior) after the 'ritual murder'.*

Greece was struggling to become independent of the Turks. The Greeks finally gained possession of the island in 1899 and Evans started work at Knossos the following spring, with thiry workmen to begin with and a Highlander called Duncan Mackenzie as his assistant. Mackenzie was an excellent linguist and skilled at keeping the records of an excavation. Evans was content to leave the day-to-day supervision of the work to him and to confine his own activities to deciding where digging should take place and to examining and assessing the finds.

He had a trained architect always on the site, which was very unusual, the common practice being to bring in an architect or surveyor at the end of the season's dig, in order to make whatever plans might be needed. At Knossos Evans used his architect for quite a different purpose as well, to reconstruct the palace as digging proceeded. This practice had its advantages – the alabaster used for interior decoration was protected from the wind and rain, and visitors to the site were able to get a good impression of how the building had originally looked – but it was certainly a luxury and it exposed Evans to the charge of spendthrift habits. He was, partly from temperament and partly as a result of his upbringing and family background, a man who was not accustomed to count the pennies. His method of proceeding at Knossos was entirely in accordance with his general style.

Criticism came both from the public and from his own colleagues. D. G. Hogarth[12] in particular spoke and wrote his mind. The Cretan Excavation Fund had been started under the auspices of the British School at Athens and it helped to finance Hogarth's sites on the island as well as Evans'. Hogarth had no private means and was obliged to draw a modest salary and his expenses from the Fund, whereas Evans, who was comfortably off and under no compulsion to earn his living, took only part of his expenses. It was an interesting and symbolic clash between two life-styles and almost two social classes. British archaeology had been created by men of leisure; Hogarth represented the new, and as yet rare breed of professionals. Evans seems to have found it difficult to understand Hogarth's position. He 'always felt about a man who made his living out of excavation rather as a mystic feels about a man who makes a living, however honourably, out of religion'.[13]

In 1902 Hogarth wrote to Evans in terms which make the letter a classic for anyone who is seeking to place the development of archaeology within its historical perspective.

> I did not intend to imply 'disapprobation' of your methods. I certainly did not express it and you must have indulged in the dangerous practice of reading between the lines. Restorations like the Throne Room are not a question of methods, but of the gratifying of a desire to reconstruct tangibly what must otherwise be only imagined. But you justly admit it is a luxury which everyone cannot pay for, and perhaps others can hardly be

expected to pay for.

These expensive methods are yours in digging, as in collecting and in ordinary life. You are a rich man's son, and have probably never been at a loss for money. At the other pole to you stands Petrie – I see advantages in the methods of both. If you spend more in proportion than Petrie, you produce far worthier results in published form, and one feels that nothing has been spared to obtain expert accuracy. One can't feel that with P's roughly drawn plans and illustrations; nor again does he leave a site so that it is a gain for the spectator. The drawback of your method is that it does not appeal to people's pockets. All P's 'cave-man' plan of life has been deliberately adopted to convince the subscriber that every penny goes into the earth. There is no doubt that unless you sue *in forma pauperis*, public subscription will not follow you. That you cannot do. You are well-known as a collector of rare and costly things, and as your father's son, and the public will not be convinced. I am not talking in the air, for I am continually chaffed about the 'princely' way things are done by us in Crete, and I have lately heard that reports about our Cretan houses, brought back, I suppose, by the big tourist parties, have decided some old subscribers not to pay up again.[14]

Hogarth was not going so far as to say that Evans' extravagance was an embarrassment and encumbrance to archaeology, since, as the letter shows, he fully recognised the value of doing things well and the need to spend sufficient money to get good results, especially where publication was concerned. What he does not seem to have realised is that both Petrie and Evans lived in their own kinds of fantasy world. On the one hand there was Petrie, with his desert asceticism, his belief in mortifying the flesh in order to clear one's mind for the truth and incidentally – Hogarth thought primarily – to attract subscriptions begging-bowl fashion, and on the other there was Evans, revelling in the colour and the beauty of Crete and in the process of discovering a new civilisation and explaining it, Apostle-like, to his fellow men. Evans found no difficulty in identifying himself with Crete and with its appeal to the senses and, in the surroundings and atmosphere of the ancient princely palace he had uncovered, it would have been perhaps natural for him to have indulged in princely dreams. We know now that these dreams led him astray and that, in order to convince the world of certain of his theories, he was guilty of falsifying archaeological evidence. It seems a pity, since the reality of what he had found was impressive enough. Was it, one wonders, that a special kind of madness overtook him, in which he fell victim to the legends and theories he had been instrumental in creating? Or was it that he had been driven on throughout his life by a constant determination to achieve more than his father had achieved, to receive a great share of public acclamation and reward?

22. *Sir Flinders Petrie on site at Memphis.*

It may be that, without, so far as one knows, being in any way aware of the archaeological deception, his daughter had found the key to his inconsistencies when she wrote of him that 'he lived as the genius he was; and a genius is a man whose mind works in so unusual a fashion that his truth to that vital working must be the only criterion of his life'.[15] But it could be also that the strangest and most charismatic of all Victorian archaeologists, Heinrich Schliemann, the discoverer of Troy, was the root of the trouble, if trouble it can be called. Evans may have envied Schliemann's extraordinary renown and success and determined at all costs to go one better. Evans was in his early twenties when reports of Schliemann's discoveries began to appear in the Press, and long afterwards he remembered the deep impression this had made on him. He wrote:

> I am old enough to recall the first authentic accounts that Schliemann sent to *The Times* of his discoveries at Mycenae, and the intense interest they aroused. I had the happiness later to make his personal acquaintance on the fields of his glory, and I still remember the echoes of his visits to England, which were his greatest scenes of triumph. . . . Something of the romance of his earlier years still seemed to cling to his personality, and I

have myself an almost uncanny memory of the spare, slightly built man, of sallow complexion and somewhat darkly clad, wearing spectacles of foreign make, through which – so the fancy took me – he had looked deep into the ground.[16]

'Romance', 'scenes of triumph', 'fields of glory' – these phrases did not come to Evans by accident. What one archaeologist had achieved by exploring the remains of ancient civilisations around the Mediterranean, another could. He too might 'look deep into the ground'.

Schliemann was a journalist's and a biographer's dream. It is curious that no-one has so far thought fit to make a film about him. This was the archaeologist-God, the excavator with everything. It is small wonder that other Victorian archaeologists with ambitions found him not only an inspiration but a perpetual challenge. For many years he was hero-worshipped to a degree which now seems more than faintly absurd and invested with a degree of glamour and mystery that did him less than justice. Adoration of Schliemann not infrequently led to ridiculous consequences. Evans, for instance, felt obliged to remark that he was 'wearing spectacles of foreign make'. What on earth does this mean? Is the reader to understand that the great man was wearing spectacles not made in England? If so, the fact was hardly surprising, since Schliemann was a Russian of German extraction. But, in any case, how did Evans know where the spectacles were made? Were they of such outrageous appearance that no Englishman would have been seen dead wearing them? Or are we to imagine the young visitor asking, 'Excuse me, sir. Could you tell me, please, where your spectacles were made? Or, for that matter, your somewhat dark clothes.' All this, of course, is simply iconoclastic. Schliemann had to be seen – and Evans was not alone in this – as a strangely intriguing figure, a man not like other men, and the glasses were just an item from the cloak-and-dagger property box.

What makes Schliemann really important is not the mystery-man-with-superhuman-powers nonsense, but his rôle as a bridge between the old world of centuries of Greek and Roman studies – literary and linguistic studies – and the new world of archaeology. Just as Botta and Layard helped to bring the biblical world alive and to make it real in a new way, so Schliemann made it possible for the familiar heroes and villains of classical times to leap from the printed page. His highly dramatic life made it easier for him to perform this function. He was a man nobody was likely to overlook and, because of the part he played in vitalising archaeology and in bringing it to public attention, it is worth spending a little time discussing him, in a book which concentrates on the achievements of the British archaeologists. Schliemann was in the atmosphere. One could not escape him, and, as in the case of all popular heroes, a vast amount of nonsense was talked and written about him. The Schliemann legend, like the Wellington legend, the Julius Caesar legend or

23. *Sir Max Mallowan.*

the Queen Victoria legend, was composed quite as much of what people wanted to believe as of the facts as they really were.

The facts themselves are interesting enough. He was a self-made man, born in 1822 in Germany at Neu Buckow, where his father was a Lutheran pastor. He left school at fourteen, went to work for a local grocer and then moved into commerce in Amsterdam and in Russia. He made a fortune in the Californian gold-rush, before returning to St Petersburg, where he amassed enormous wealth from Russian railways, Greek olive oil, American cotton, Cuban sugar and South American hemp. He was a profiteer on the grand scale in the Crimean War and the American Civil War and by the time he was forty-one he had all the money he needed to give him financial security for the rest of his life and to make it possible for him to fulfil his life-dream – or, rather, what he said had been his life-dream – to discover and excavate the site of Troy.

For this he required a Greek wife, who would resemble as nearly as possible Helen of Troy as he visualised her. She was selected by correspondence, through the good offices of an Athenian archbishop who had been a theological student in St Petersburg and who had tutored Schliemann in ancient and modern Greek, in preparation for his great venture. Having divorced his Russian wife, as a necessary preliminary step, he said farewell to Russia and his family and transferred himself to the Mediterranean. Before starting work, he took his young wife on a whirlwind tour of Italy, Germany and France, immersing her in museums and talking unceasingly about archaeology. Not surprisingly, this period of intensive basic education made her ill.

The honeymoon having been completed to his satisfaction, if not altogether that of his wife, he settled down at Hissarlik, on the Turkish coast, having decided from his interpretation of Homer that this was the site of Troy, a conclusion absolutely at variance with that of most other scholars. To prepare himself for his major task, he had already carried out excavations at Ithaca, at Mycenae in the Peloponnese – he went back there after conpleting his work at Troy – and at two sites in Asia Minor. In 1870 he carried out a trial excavation at Hissarlik, without official permission, and then, convinced that he was digging in the right place, settled down to finding the details of Troy.

The Schliemanns lived on the site, not uncomfortably, except that they were tormented by insects and kept awake by a plague of owls. The owls, Schliemann later discovered, had been there since Homeric times, and the tutelary goddess of Troy, the Ilian Athena, had an owl's face. Discipline was autocratic. On one occasion seventy workers were summarily dismissed for disobeying instructions that there was to be no smoking during working hours.

Schliemann, helped by continual bribes, usually managed to outwit the

Turks and to arrange matters to his satisfaction. He achieved a particularly rewarding triumph in 1873, when he succeeded in smuggling away to Athens the great treasure-hoard he had discovered that summer. The Trojan collections, which had spent some years in London, eventually went to Berlin.

Everything the Schliemanns did was carried out in great style. Their two children were named, inevitably, Andromache and Agamemnon, and the palace they built for themselves in the middle of Athens, 'Iliou Melathron', was the largest private residence in the city. For his lecture to the Society of Antiquaries in London in 1877, he took enormous pains with his appearance.[17] Dressed in a frock coat, with a white tie, he wore a collar much lower than that displayed by the Fellows who had come to listen to him. This was to make his short neck look longer and to give the illusion of greater height. His suits, shoes, hats and shirts were always made in London, to his own exacting specification. At one time he thought fit to mention that his wardrobe contained fifty suits, twenty hats, forty-two pairs of shoes, thirty walking-sticks and fifteen riding crops. His valet, who travelled with him, kept everything in perfect condition.

The Victorians were great snobs or, to use gentler language, they admired people who behaved in accordance with their social status. Schliemann was extremely obliging in this respect. He behaved as an archaeological prince was expected to behave and archaeology gained in prestige accordingly. It would be wrong, however, to allow the ludicrous aspects of Schliemann's career to obscure his great talents and the considerable contribution he made to the development of a more fruitful approach. One has to say 'more fruitful', rather than 'more scientific', because one of his great merits, perhaps his greatest, was his ability to make intuition part of his method. Having almost reached the right answer by means of a highly intelligent interpretation of the existing written evidence, he was in a position to clinch the matter through excavation. One could say, of course, that the task was made easier for him by choosing a civilisation and a part of the world for which written evidence existed. How easy or how greatly to his taste he would have found excavating, say, a neolithic site, or a site in Egypt, where there was no literature and no records and the archaeology represented the whole of the evidence, it is impossible to say. Without Homer to quicken his imagination and to tell him what was to be done, he might quite well have contented himself with making a fortune.

That he inspired other archaeologists there can be no doubt at all. Sir Arthur Evans was perhaps an inevitable disciple. Both men understood and sympathised with extravagance and flamboyance, both greatly enjoyed the politics of archaeology in the areas controlled by the Turks, both found enormous pleasure in the Mediterranean itself. But archaeologists of a much more solid and sober kind learned a great deal from the meetings with

24. *Lord Carnarvon and Howard Carter on site at the tomb of Tutankhamun.*

Schliemann and from reading about his work. Sir John Lubbock, for instance, corresponded with Schliemann and spent weeks on the site of Troy with him, watching him at work and listening to him with great interest and enthusiasm as he developed his theories. Lubbock was fond of telling his friends that, although desk-bound scholars had been arguing for years as to where the site of Troy was, each supporting his ideas with quotations from Homer, Schliemann took the step they refused to take – he went to the spot and dug until he found the stones of Troy. This essential difference between the traditional scholar and the field-worker made a deep impression on Lubbock and, as he was never ashamed to admit, greatly influenced his own work.

Schliemann was a great showman and so, too, was the man who was to become, at least in Britain, the most famous of all the Near Eastern excavators, Sir Leonard Woolley, discoverer of the treasures at Ur of the Chaldees. In all other ways, however, two more different people it would have been hard to find. Woolley had no fortune and no burning sense of mission. He was short of money all his life and he blundered into archaeology because he needed to find some way of making a living.

> I have seldom been more surprised that I was when – it is nearly fifty years ago – the Warden of New College told me that he had decided that I should be an archaeologist. It is true that I had taken a course in Greek sculpture for my degree, but so had lots of undergraduates. Because of the bearing on Homer, I had read Schliemann's romantic account of his discoveries, the Treasure of Priam at Troy and the Tomb of Agamemnon at Mycenae, and like everyone else I was vaguely aware that Flinders Petrie was, year after year, making history in Egypt and that Arthur Evans was unearthing the Palace of Minos in Crete, but all this was at best only background knowledge and the idea of making a life study of it had never occurred to me.[18]

He worked for a while at the Ashmolean, as Assistant Keeper, and was then put in charge of an excavation at the Roman station at Corbridge, in Northumberland. At that time he had no experience of field archaeology whatever and, since there were no books on archaeological methods, no idea as to how to set about the task. But the *Victoria County History for Northumberland* was being written and the editors wanted the kind of information about Corbridge that only some sort of excavation could supply, so the Ashmolean let them have Woolley. He was supplied with nine labourers and, with their help, he acquired experience that was afterwards to be of the greatest benefit to him in Mesopotamia.

> Our men, mostly coal-miners, had taken on the job simply for want of a

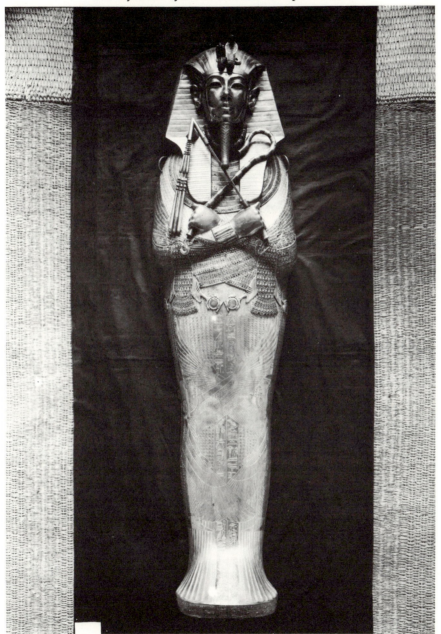

25. *Archaeology at its most glamorous. Gold tomb figure found in the tomb of Tutan-khamun.*

better, and, at the start, did not disguise the fact that they thought it rather silly and certainly not one that called for hard work. Gradually, by dint of explaining and discussing things, we got them to understand what we were after, and in proportion as they became keen their work got better and before the season ended we had a really fine gang.

Archaeological digging requires a lot of skill and skill directed by intelligence. This does not mean that the labourers supply the skill and the director the intelligence – which simply would not work – but that the two qualities should be shared by all alike. The men are not just 'hands', they are fellow workers.[19]

One can hardly imagine Pitt-Rivers, Arthur Evans or Schliemann writing in this way, although Petrie could have done. But times had changed and by the time Woolley became seriously involved in excavations there were not many of the old type of masterful, rich, autocratic diggers around in Britain. They were essentially a Victorian phenomenon. Near Eastern archaeology had in any case become very much an international pursuit, with an interesting mixture of different styles of work and sources of finance. This was particularly true of Egypt. Until the turn of the century the British and the French had the field to themselves, but from then onwards the Americans, Germans, Italians, Belgians and Poles all carried out excavations there. During the 1914–18 War German activity in Egypt, conducted through the well-financed Deutsche Orient-Gesellschaft,[20] necessarily came to a standstill and the British and French, too, had more pressing things than archaeology to think about. But, with the war over, British archaeology in Egypt soon entered its most spectacular, if not its scientifically most important phase, with the work of the Egypt Exploration Society and the British School of Archaeology in Egypt. The discoveries at Tell el-Amaina, which allowed archaeologists to reconstruct an exceptionally detailed picture of life in the fourteenth century BC, followed in 1923 by the excavation of Tutankhamun's tomb by Howard Carter and Lord Carnarvon brought Egypt back into the limelight in a dramatic way, to a public which was very receptive to excitement of this kind. The machinations, ambitions and jealousies of Carter and Carnarvon and their careful stage-management, not to say falsification, of the circumstances of the discovery of the tomb are a matter of personal, rather than social history, except in so far as a desire for glory is a fairly common human failing and archaeologists have no immunity from the general British yearning for titles. As a profession, they probably received their fair share of knighthoods up to 1939, but since then they have not, for some reason or combination of reasons, done quite so well.

What caught the popular fancy about the Tutankhamun discoveries was the quantity of gold and jewellery that was unearthed. Tutankhamun became

26. *Alabaster vase from the tomb of Tutankhamun.*

identified in the public mind with treasure and with beautiful objects. The movement around the world of the finest of these objects during the past decade – the exhibition has been an enormous success wherever it has gone, East and West of the Iron Curtain – proves what perhaps needed no proving, that there is nothing like gold and jewels for drawing the crowds. A pleasant aspect of this royal progress has been that it has yielded a handsome income to the impoverished National Museum in Cairo, from which the treasures came.

Howard Carter and Lord Carnarvon were much concerned with personal glory and received their full measure of it, but they were not in the top class as popularisers. The appeal of what one might term the Tutankhamun affair came from the nature of the discoveries themselves, and from the literally golden opportunity they presented to journalists. It is frightening to think what television would have made of it all, but, mercifully, the Royal Tomb was found in pre-television days.

Ur of the Chaldees was quite another matter. Woolley was a populariser of the highest quality and, unlike Carter and Carnarvon, he needed the money. He had appealing personal qualities – a lean, boyish, weather-beaten, sun-tanned appearance and a modest manner – and he happened, too, to be an exceptionally talented raconteur. He had the other great advantage of being linked with a man who enjoyed a remarkable reputation as a popular hero during the 1920s and 1930s, T. E. Lawrence, 'Lawrence of Arabia'. Those were the days before Arabia was identified with oil and when Arabs were still thought of as romantic figures.

Woolley had become a confirmed Arabist before the First World War. He was fully at home in the area and got on well with Arabs. He was also politically very useful to the British Government, which in turn was prepared to be of assistance to him in his archaeological work. In the Near East, the dividing line between politics and archaeology has always been very thin and often unreal. Some part of Woolley's success must undoubtedly be attributed to the fact that he was a highly accomplished politician and intelligence agent, as well as a skilful archaeologist. He is by no means the only British archaeologist of whom this could be said. An interesting feature of the history of archaeology and archaeologists is the ease with which they moved during two World Wars from their professional work to military intelligence and as easily back again. This, however would be the subject of another book.

At all events, Leonard Woolley became the second Director of the Egypt Exploration Society, in the early Twenties, and then, in 1922, was offered the chance of transferring his attentions to Mesopotamia. Before 1914, the Deutsche Orient Gesellschaft had carried out a number of important excavations in this inhospitable area, where there was little to think about, apart from the heat and one's work. At Babylon and Assur they were the first to reveal the ruins of any Babylonian or Assyrian town, although earlier surveys had made it clear that the area had very great archaeological potential. As early as 1854, the British Consul at Basra, J. E. Taylor, had been employed by the British Museum to investigate sites in the southern part of Mesopotamia. He concentrated his attentions on the Mound of Pitch, the Ziggurat hill at Ur, half-way between Baghdad and the head of the Persian Gulf. Here he discovered inscriptions which made it clear that the Mound of Pitch was the site of Ur, the home of Abraham. Through lack of funds and because of the dangerous nature of the district, Taylor could work for only two seasons. In the 1890s the University of Pennsylvania sent an expedition to Ur, but it accomplished very little, and nothing further happened there until the First World War brought British troops into Mesopotamia. The archaeologists followed in the wake of the soldiers. In 1918 R. Campbell Thompson, who had been on the staff of the British Museum and was at that time a member of British Military Intelligence, carried out trial excavations at both Eridu and Ur. The British Museum sent out an expedition soon afterwards, but, although it was able to confirm Campbell Thompson's assessment of the importance of the site, had to cease operations because no further money was available. In 1922, however, it was

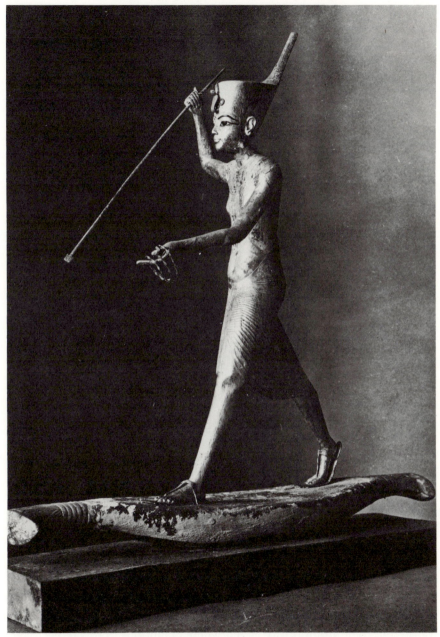

27. *More excitement from Egypt. Figurine from the tomb of Tutankhamun.*

possible to organise a joint British Museum/University of Pennsylvania Expedition and Woolley was appointed to lead it.

Woolley worked at Ur and Al'Ubaid for seven winters and in 1926 discovered the great cemetery at Ur, with its so-called Royal Tombs, with their wonderful treasures of gold and lapis lazuli. Ur of the Chaldees then took its place among the great archaeological sites of which nearly everyone had heard, along with Mycenae, Troy, and Tutankhamun's tomb. The entry of Ur into the public repertoire was due partly to the nature of the finds – once again, successful archaeologist had been equated with successful treasure-hunter – but even more to Woolley's skill in writing up his work in a way which would appeal to the general reader. He had the power to communicate his own excitement and, as a natural story-teller, he was not in the least ashamed to do so. Here is an example, from *Ur of the Chaldees*.

We dug deeper down, and suddenly limestone blocks appeared, bedded in green clay and forming a curve; we took it to be the end of a stone vault, and when the stones quickly dipped again feared that the roof had been broken through by robbers; but another half-hour's work proved, to our delight, that the masonry continued and that what we had was a small dome absolutely intact. It was particularly exciting because the top of the dome had been built over a centring supported by stout beams which ran right through the stone-work, and the decay of these had left half a dozen holes in the roof through which one could glimpse parts of the dim interior and by the light of electric torches could even see on the floor below the shapes of green copper vessels and catch an occasional glint of gold.[21]

Ur of the Chaldees was published in 1929 and went through eight editions between then and 1935. It reached an even larger market when it appeared as one of the early Pelican paperbacks in 1938, the first book on archaeology to be so honoured. *The Sumerians* followed in 1930 and *Abraham, Recent Discoveries and Hebrew Origins* in 1936. Full and scholarly accounts of the excavations were published in six volumes between 1928 and 1938. Woolley's pattern of life over these years was very regular and very fruitful, digging in Mesopotamia in the winter and writing up the results in England during the rest of the year.

One should not overlook the fact that until the Thirties it was possible for archaeologists in Mesopotamia, that is, Iraq, to remove the whole of their finds from the country. In 1933, however, the Iraq Government passed a law forbidding the export of antiquities, at which point the British and French transferred their attentions to Syria, where conditions in this respect were more to their liking.

It is interesting to observe that Woolley was a disciple of Petrie in the matter of carrying out excavations as cheaply as possible. He wrote:

28. *Sir Arthur Evans at Knossos.*

One is in duty bound to make the most economical use of one's archaeological fund, which is meant for digging and ought to be employed on digging, so far as possible, directly; while there are all sorts of 'overhead expenses', such as equipment and travelling, about two-thirds of the total spent ought to go on wages to the men. But the work of the staff is no less essential, and men cannot do their best work unless they are well fed and reasonably comfortable. Anything imported is certain to be expensive, but one can live well and cheaply if one makes proper use of local produce and sees to it that it is well cooked; and a house, adequate but not luxurious, should represent a real saving of money. Our Carchemish house (planned for a ten-years dig) was of rough stone collected from the site, and mud-brick, one storey high, with a flat roof made native fashion of earth spread over poles and matting.[22]

Sir Max Mallowan, who worked at Ur with Woolley and at Nineveh with Campbell Thompson, congratulated himself in his autobiography on his good fortune in having been active during what Sir Frederick Kenyon once described as the Elizabethan Age of Archaeology. Mallowan's comparison between the Twenties and Thirties on the one hand and the Seventies on the other is both a fitting valediction to the old romantic days, of which he was proud and happy to have been a part, and the new scientific period, which contains a higher degree of compromise and adaptation than its protagonists would care to admit. It has not, Mallowan feels, been all gain. He writes:

In the Orient we had, at least for the first three decades of my career, both the time and the financial resources in the grand manner, on a grand scale. Thirty years ago, when you could hire a man's services for a shilling a day, it was not unusual for big expeditions to work with a labour force which not infrequently numbered two hundred or more, with only a small supervisory staff. Ur was the classic example of work conducted on this scale. In the course of twelve years of digging, over periods which sometimes amounted to five months, many hundreds of thousands of tons of soil were shifted, and the evidence was of a high order of magnitude and ranged over a period of some six thousand years. The catalogue register numbered some twenty thousand objects, which will be studied and re-examined for as long as Mesopotamian archaeology is deemed worthy of attention – perhaps for eternity – and, with the growth of knowledge, interpretation and re-interpretation will succeed one another generation after generation.

But inevitably, because of the speed at which operations were conducted, a not inconsiderable volume of evidence was lost, and that in spite of much brilliant field-work which could hold its own by any standards. However, had we worked on excavations by the canons which are accepted today, we should have recovered but one-tenth of the evidence, and the other nine-tenths would probably never have been found. I am therefore, on balance, an unashamed supporter of the bygone days of digging – the last of 'the Romantics', as a colleague in Indian archaeology has been good enough to dub me. But given the restrictions of our present economy, no less than the development of scientific methods, we are bound to dig on a relatively modest scale and consequently to put all the evidence through a fine sieve; we therefore miss nothing, and tend to find nothing. Sometimes the evidence recovered is of so light a character that an older generation is inclined to wonder if the effort is worth while.[23]

To which one might perhaps add three comments. First, because these Near Eastern giants achieved their results by shifting hundreds of thousands of tons of soil, the word 'archaeology' took on a new and much narrower meaning than it had had previously, and this was a great pity. Second, this remarkable race of British diggers in hot and unpleasant places can be seen as a last flowering of the old imperialist tradition at its best. Under different circumstances, the Woolleys and the Mallowans might well have been excellent District Officers in India or the Sudan, with the same task of putting up with physical difficulties, getting the best out of the natives and administering justice and fair treatment all round. And, thirdly, that Mallowan's remark about modern archaeologists tending to miss nothing and find nothing is more than a witty epigram. It is an acute criticism of a great deal of today's grotesquely over-specialised research in every academic field. At one time scholars carried out research into Shakespeare's attitude to death or to power; now the Ph.D. subject is much more likely to be the use of the indefinite article in Act I of *Macbeth*, or its archaeological equivalent.

4 Cultivating the Public

There are two basic reasons why any profession or group of experts should feel it necessary to cultivate the general public and to obtain its goodwill. One is to extract money from it and the other is on order to create the kind of atmosphere in which it is easier to do the work one wants to do in the way in which one wants to do it. For both these purposes, the public, or such sections of it that one feels to be significant, can be flattered, bullied, frightened or reasoned with, according to the circumstances and the immediate task in hand. At different times, archaeologists, like doctors, lawyers, politicians and commercial firms, have used all four types of approach, often in combination, although what they were doing has by no means always been recognised for what it was. An appeal to snobbery, for instance, almost always contains fairly strong elements of both flattery and bullying. The person or body responsible is saying, in effect: 'You are a special kind of person – rich, influential, powerful, unusually intelligent, highly educated, or whatever quality seems most relevant and useful – and, as a matter of group solidarity, you have a duty, or, alternatively, you would naturally wish, to support us in this way. If you fail to support us, people may not feel that you are a worthy member of the social group to which you are so proud to belong. If, on the other hand, you do support us, people will continue to think well of you and your reputation and prestige may even increase.' This, or something very like it, was the basis of most fund-raising before the First World War and a great deal since then. There is nothing cynical about such an analysis; it is common sense, and, without it, excavation funds would never have produced any money, the County Archaeological Societies would have had practically no members and specialist periodicals would have found it extremely difficult to get off the ground, and to survive. One is relying to a large extent on group solidarity, and all that is normally necessary is a skilful but tactful reminder to one's victim of the social group to which he or she belongs. All that is then required is the traditional British response of not letting one's side down.

A problem arises, however, when an interest-group is being created or defined for the first time. In 1871, *The Antiquarian* described itself as 'a fortnightly medium of intercommunication for archaeologists, antiquarians, numismatists, the virtuosi and collectors of articles of virtù', and in this way suggested that there was a substantial measure of common interest between these different categories of person, and that they might like to consider themselves a more or less cohesive group, all, in fact, antiquarians, people devoted to the study of objects surviving from the past.

With the group defined, what was then needed was a manifesto, a statement of philosophy, motivation and intention. *The Antiquarian* set it out in this form.

> We know that the human mind is adapted to contemplate the Past as well as the Present and the Future, and that, without a knowledge of the Past, most of the facts of present life are incomprehensible. Nay, all power of regulating the future comes from a knowledge of the present state of things, gained by a knowledge of the past. The province of the antiquarian is the Past, especially the remote Past, extending backwards to the earliest records or to the objects fabricated by man in prehistoric times. By laborious industry in collecting facts relating to ancient objects and ancient manners, and by their comparisons, he is able to arrive at general ideas which explain present matters and which may be used by the philosopher for the regulation of the future. It is a law thoroughly established that the best way to attain a perfect knowledge of any subject is by bringing all matters related thereto under consideration and starting an average or general principle in consideration as a whole. The archaeologist and the antiquarian is not, therefore, the useless person that is sometimes thoughtlessly portraited, but a valuable contributor to the world's progress.'[1]

This was an intelligent approach. In any age, most people like to be considered useful members of society, and in the quotation given above there is a strong suggestion that the general public might be regarding antiquarians somewhat as fringe members of society, people who passed their time agreeably but selfishly, making no real contribution to the general welfare, mere drones. To assure them that their tastes and habits were to the advantage of mankind was to raise their morale, both individually and as a group, and to remind them that by co-operating, and incidentally subscribing to *The Antiquarian*, which was their friend and defender, they would make it more likely that this important truth would become more widely realised.

One does not know who bought and read *The Antiquarian* and, in the absence of any reliable evidence, one can only assume that the subscribers were the kind of people the editor had in mind and described when he launched the paper. There seems little doubt that they were members of a class which might be termed either amateurs or connoisseurs, men and much less frequently women who had a hobby interest in these things and who

29. *Dr Mortimer Wheeler's methods at Maiden Castle in the 1930s. Parties being taken round the site in 1936. The grid pattern of the excavation provided convenient walkways for ladies and the elderly and infirm, so that, on a fine day, a visit to Maiden Castle could be a very agreeable occasion. The parties were small and the guides were briefed to give knowledgeable and courteous attention.*

might well have been similar in many ways to the people who have bought and enjoyed *Country Life* for the past half-century, and who write letters to this periodical about objects in their possession. They are unlikely to have included very many professionals, who earned a living as dealers in coins, antiques or works of art, and there were clearly quite a lot of them, since the magazine prospered for more than twenty-five years and lasted well into the present century. Most of them were probably collectors of one kind or another. Some, but not many, may have been Fellows of the Society of Antiquaries.

But, whoever its readers may have been, its market seems to have largely died away by the time of the First World War, by which time there were better produced weeklies and monthlies with photographic illustrations available, although at a higher price, and a more marked tendency for enthusiastic collectors to buy publications which were confined to their special interests.

Until O. G. S. Crawford founded *Antiquity* in 1925, there was no periodical devoted entirely to archaeology to which anybody could subscribe.

The *Antiquaries Journal* was something quite different. It was essentially and as a matter of policy the house-journal of the Society of Antiquaries. Fellows received it automatically, as one of the consequences and rewards of their election. The general public could not buy it, although they could, if they wanted to, read it in some of the larger libraries.

In order to understand what Crawford was trying to do with *Antiquity*, it is necessary to know something about the career and background of this remarkable man.[2] He was born in Bombay, where his father was a judge. At Marlborough, which he loathed, he joined the Archaeological Section of the Natural History Society. When he was an undergraduate at Oxford, he helped to excavate the Ham Barrow on the Marlborough Downs, and this led him to make the acquaintance of Harald Peake and his wife, who lived nearby at Boxford. Partly as a result of their influence, Crawford gave up Greats at Oxford and took the Geography Diploma, having made up his mind that he wanted 'to study pre-history against the background of a geographical environment', since 'archaeology as then taught at Oxford was confined to the study of classical sculpture and Greek vases'.

After a number of attempts to find a satisfactory niche for himself on the excavation side of archaeology, he went to work, in 1920, for the Ordnance Survey, as its first Archaeology Officer. In this post, he developed his techniques of air-photography and published *Wessex from the Air* in 1928.

In establishing *Antiquity* and in the development of his philosophy of archaeology, he was greatly influenced by the writings and friendship of Gordon Childe. Archaeology, he said, was concerned with 'the development of the human race and of the various forms of civilisation which it has evolved'. Looking back from the vantage point of 1936, when the fortieth issue of *Antiquity* appeared, he recalled what his aim had been eleven years earlier. 'What I had in mind,' he wrote, 'was to found a journal which would raise the general status of archaeology, and would popularise its achievements without vulgarising them – in a word, which would take a place equivalent (both in form and content) to that already occupied by the monthlies and quarterlies in regard to public affairs generally. The main outlines for the evolution of human culture are now firmly established, and it was time that this knowledge should become diffused. Here was demand without a supply. I decided to meet it.'[3]

Since his concern was with 'the development of the human race', and not with any particular section of it, Crawford's policy was to cover the world. The titles of the main articles in a typical issue[4] were:

'The Coming of Iron'
'Pits and Pit-dwellings in South-east Europe'
'Roman Barrows'
'Easter Island, Polynesia'

'Anglo-Saxon Vine-scroll Ornament'
'The Cyclopean Walls at Tarragona'
'Some Recent Excavations in Egypt'

This geographical and subject range was maintained by Crawford through-out the long periods of his editorship and it has been continued by his successor, Glyn Daniel. Yet *Antiquity* has never achieved a world circulation of more than 5,000 copies, which makes it difficult for one to say that it has, in any reasonable sense of the word, 'popularised' archaeology, although it has certainly not 'vulgarised' it. There are a number of probable reasons for this. The first, and the most important, is that the editors have been on the whole more anxious to gain the good opinion of scholars than of the general public. Mainly for this reason, the appearance of the publication is unmistakably that of a learned journal, an impression which is confirmed by the style of writing, by the character of the illustrations and by the layout. It is not that the subjects of the articles are uninteresting, nor that the authors write badly. The failing, given Crawford's intention to found a popular journal, is that the form and flavour of *Antiquity* immediately suggest to the average person who is interested or, even more important, who is capable of being interested in Roman barrows, Easter Island or excavation in Egypt that this particular publication is really intended for someone else. It does not resemble the other weeklies or monthlies which normally come his way, and it suffers from the great disadvantage of having none of its illustrations in colour, which is nowadays a serious defect, although it was much less so before the war. In addition to this, the precedent established by Crawford of making it available only by subscription was bound to damn its chances of becoming a truly popular venture. It was not possible to buy an odd copy at a bookstall and taste it to discover if it was to one's liking.

To be a successful populariser is a very rare gift, and it is doubtful if Crawford possessed it. It demands the ability to tell a story and to imagine an audience and to make frequent use of the word 'I', and the willingness and the skill to go to the heart of a matter and to jettison most of the apparatus of qualifications and references so beloved by academics and so baffling and infuriating to nearly everyone else. Sir Leonard Woolley had this gift and the result was that books like *Ur of the Chaldees* were what the critics, having no better word to hand, are accustomed to call 'readable' or, in exceptional cases, 'very readable'. The populariser has to be 'readable', that is, he must write as if he were speaking, always mentally thinking of his readers as if they were listeners, watching to see if they are still interested and paying attention. He must have the experience to know that all writing and speaking, to be fully effective, needs light and shade, the chance to rest, pause and perhaps smile between moments of concentration, the occasional touch of drama and excitement. None of this implies vulgarisation; all of it

30. *The public relations value of the macabre. Knowing that nothing succeeds as well as a skeleton, Dr Wheeler displayed his Maiden Castle graves with brilliant showmanship.*

belongs to popularisation. It is interesting to wonder what a popular archaeological journal edited by Woolley would have been like and how he would have faced up to the task. In all probability he would have despaired of the woodenness and flatness of most of the articles submitted to him, found it impossible to teach his contributors to talk their material, instead of write it, and given up in torment after a couple of years. An editor who is better than most of his contributors is in a wretched situation, since he cannot write everything himself, or even drastically rewrite it.

One has to be very careful when using words like 'popular' or 'popularise', because they clearly mean quite different things to different people. A specialist whose book sells a thousand copies has often done remarkably well as to lay himself open to attacks which are all too likely to make use of such damning expressions as 'charlatan' or 'lacking in seriousness', whereas a television programme which is watched by only a million people can easily be labelled 'élitist' or 'minority taste'. The fact is that, by any standard that makes sense, there was hardly any 'popularisation' of archaeology before the 1940s, and in some respects there was even less in the 1920s and 1930s than there had been fifty years earlier. *The Antiquarian* had no equivalent between the wars.

The person who is commonly reckoned to have done more than anyone else to make archaeology popular in Britain is the late Sir Mortimer Wheeler. It may be true, but the claim and the evidence for it deserve careful examination. That Wheeler deliberately set out to cultivate, inform and win over the public is not in doubt, but whether everyone else was quite such a dwarf by comparison is open to question. Let us begin our investigation into Mortimer Wheeler, the great impresario of archaeology, with one or two informed eulogies. First, A. J. Taylor, in his Presidential address to the Antiquaries in 1976. Reporting Wheeler's death, he said:

Wheeler was the foremost archaeologist of our time. His influence was worldwide. Through the novelty of television his vivid personality brought the highlights of archaeology into every home in the land; and if the name Mortimer Wheeler became a household word, archaeology became synonymous with it. What had been the preserve of scholars was being disseminated among laymen and the younger generation by none other than the voted television personality of the year. There can be little doubt that the phenomenal widening of popular interest in archaeology . . . owed more to this combination of circumstances than to any other single factor.[5]

Second, Sir Max Mallowan:

Mortimer Wheeler, or Rik, as he was familiarly known to his many friends, was a monument and always looked like one. This megalith of a man, an over-engined dynamo, strode through life breathing fire, a fire which either burned opposition or was miraculously cleansing, a process of cauterisation which healed and reanimated. He was possessed of the kind of genius which my old master, Leonard Woolley, was endowed: namely that whatever he touched came to life, whether it was the Institute of Archaeology, the British Academy or Mohenjo Daro.

No man was more effective in Committee and it was as Secretary of the British Academy, an organisation that he reorganised and transformed, that he could be seen playing his most forceful role. Always histrionic, he was born to hold the stage and in the Presidential Chair at the Antiquities (sic) Society he looked like King Lear; his presence was overwhelming. At the British Academy, where he exercised plenary powers, he was seen at his best because he knew exactly what he wanted. He had a quick and alert mind which was repaid in action and gave little thought to diplomacy; he never wore kid gloves. When an assembly was locked in debate, his authority was ever ready to cut the Gordian knot. He was a rare combination of artist and practical man of affairs. As an artist, he was a leading figure of his time in the world of television and no one will forget him as a *tour de force* on the programme entitled *Animal, Vegetable, Mineral,* ably sponsored by Glyn Daniel, who was the impresario. From this it follows that he was not everybody's cup of tea and that there were persons who could not abide him.[6]

The last point is certainly true. Short men hated Wheeler, who had a remarkable knack of making them feel inferior; and, on the whole, there were more men than women who disliked him. But this, although not without it importance, is not greatly relevant to the present point, which is concerned with his image with the general public and the way in which he used that image to make people more interested in archaeology. The key phrases from the passages by Taylor and Mallowan make it clear what that image was – 'vivid personality', 'television personality of the year', 'megalith of a man', 'over-engined dynamo', 'genius', 'histrionic', 'never wore kid gloves'. He was indeed God's gift to television, a medium to which he was perfectly suited. *Animal, Vegetable, Mineral* was one of the great successes of the Fifties, with a six year run to its credit. During the same decade he also achieved remarkable popularity in the *Buried Treasure* series, in which he was partnered by Glyn Daniel. The two leading television archaeologists described, in a number of programmes, a wide range of archaeological discoveries in various parts of the world, and the public liked what they saw and heard.

But, and this cannot be said too strongly, there is all the difference in the world between popularising archaeology and making archaeology popular. The first is concerned with helping people to learn and the second with getting them interested and, in a small proportion of cases, with persuading them to learn. Wheeler did a small amount of the first and a very great deal of the second. Having decided that television was to be his major public relations tool, it was inevitable that Wheeler should be a man who made archaeology popular, not a populariser. The reason for this lies in the nature of the medium; television, in the right hands, is a splendid tool for arousing interest and weakening prejudice; it is a very poor tool for real learning, an activity in which the printed word is still supreme.

It was in the course of his memorable Maiden Castle excavation in the years immediately preceding the Second World War that Sir Mortimer Wheeler's talents for organising and handling public relations and publicity really developed,[7] and it was largely because his wife, Tessa, took most of the supervision of the practical aspects of the dig off his shoulders that he was able to concentrate on building up links of all kinds with the public. She had done exactly the same on previous sites, and Wheeler was very dependent on her in this respect. She died suddenly in 1936 and once the work at Maiden Castle had been finished it is significant that he never undertook another dig on his own account. Tessa Wheeler has not received the proper recognition

31. *Watching the natives at work. This markedly middle-class party of visitors at Maiden Castle is able to see how the main rampart was excavated under Dr Wheeler's supervision.*

due to her for her indispensable rôle in her husband's archaeological work, especially at Verulamium and Maiden Castle. She looked after all the day-to-day activities on the site and was always there, leaving him free to come and go as he pleased and as his other duties demanded. One of her great merits was the attention she paid to the welfare and instruction of students working on the site. 'I shall never forget her personal kindness to me,' wrote one of them, to Lt Col. C. D. Drew, Joint Organiser of the Maiden Castle project, soon after her death,[8] and there were hundreds more who could have said the same.

At Maiden Castle, as on his earlier digs, Wheeler was the front man, a task he enjoyed and carried out brilliantly well. He approached the right people for contributions to the Excavation Fund, showed distinguished visitors round the site, gave local and national lectures, and looked after every kind of publicity. But he could only manage this because other people – at Maiden Castle it was his wife and Col. Drew – could be relied on to look after the chores. And the chores were of a great many kinds, paying wages, arranging accommodation, finding suitable paid labourers, keeping the accounts and site records, dealing efficiently with the never-ending queries of letters and requests from members of the public and supporters of the Fund.'   It is useful to give a few examples of this, partly to make clear that much of the public relations work in archaeology is not of the kind that finds its way into the newspapers or, for that matter, into biographies and obituaries, and partly to illustrate the many levels on which the title of this chapter, 'Cultivating the Public', has to be studied and interpreted. This is not in any way to denigrate Sir Mortimer or other recent notable directors of excavations, or to minimise the value of their own special contribution to the enterprise in hand. It is simply to remind one's readers that running a major archaeological excavation is not unlike winning a Nobel Prize. The person who receives all the credit is the visible tip of a large iceberg. Behind him, or less frequently her, is a team of people, paid and unpaid, without whom nothing could have been achieved at all. To refer to Mortimer Wheeler's excavation at Maiden Castle' or 'Leslie Alcock's excavation at Cadbury Camp' is, in one way, as unfair and as meaningless as talking about 'Brunel's Great Western Railway' or 'Sir Alexander Fleming's discovery of penicillin'. None of these things are one-man achievements, although it is perfectly true to say that without the imagination and directing intelligence of that one man the project would never have come to fruition. It is always the old and unanswerable question, 'who needs whom most?'. But, and this point is often forgotten, the people with whom members of the general public are most likely to come into direct contact with an archaeological dig are people at a lower level than the director. The bulk of public relations work is usually not a glamorous affair at all and it is essential to make a clear distinction between public relations and publicity. The first is usually quiet and unsung, the second necessarily planned to be as widely noticed as possible.

Here, for example, is a piece of public relations, the correct and prompt handling of a lady in Windsor who had been to Maiden Castle and needed a little help as a result:

Dear Sir,

Visiting Maiden Castle last week I intended buying some sling stones which I saw were on sale. Somehow I left the excavations by a different route and missed the place where they were being sold. I had meant to procure them on my return tramp.

I should be grateful if you could send me three or so that might fit into the box I am sending with this. I have no idea of the price. I am enclosing a postal order for 3/-. If there should be any balance after paying for stones and postage, please drop it into any box for the benefit of the excavation if the Museum is in your charge.

Many congratulations on the many interesting things you have brought to light at Maiden Castle.[9]

It was not Wheeler who had to cope with this time- and labour-consuming request, but the enormously busy and ever-courteous and helpful Col. Drew, who had the Dorset County Museum and Dorset Archaeological Society to run, in addition to looking after the practical details of Maiden Castle. The lady from Windsor might be important and influential, she might not, but in either case one had a duty to make her happy, always reckoning that the reputation and possibly the finances of the dig might benefit as a result. Most people have friends and some people have a lot of friends, and the best publicity in the long run is always by word of mouth.

But there is always direct publicity and this is where Mortimer Wheeler really entered his kingdom. There were the lectures:

R. E. Mortimer Wheeler, Esq.

M.C., M.A., D.Litt., F.S.A.

Keeper of the London Museum

will give
a Lantern Lecture
on

The Excavations at Maiden Castle

in the Corn Exchange, Dorchester
on Tuesday, April 6th, 1937
at 8.30 p.m.

Tickets: 2s. 6d (Reserved); 1s (Unreserved)

The hall at the Corn Exchange would be packed out, the occasion would be reported in the local papers and, with luck, in one or two of the nationals, too, and a few pounds would be added to the Excavation Fund.

Or Dr Wheeler might plan a little secret *tour de force*:

Between ourselves and extremely privately, I am bringing down a very good man with an excellent cinema camera with a view to taking our western entrance from the front of a moving car. This is all frightfully hush hush.[10]

The film was taken and it was available to the Director for lectures and fund-raising activities as required, an admirable and characteristic piece of enterprise, in the days when the large glass slide still reigned supreme and it was fairly uncommon to make use of film in this way.

32. *Maiden Castle, 1934. Dr Wheeler's tourist altars. Towards the back of this picture, to the right of a pile of turves, one can see the end of a trestle table, with a group of visitors standing attentively behind it. Finds from the current stage of the excavation were placed on the table, to serve as visual aids for the student-guide talking to the visitors. For the male students, it should be noted, colonial-type khaki shorts were the rule: the hired labourers, doing more arduous work, wore trousers. Most, but not all, of the women wore skirts.*

And then there were the journalists. Wheeler enjoyed handling journalists and understood the nature of their job and the way in which their minds worked. His father, one should remember, had been a journalist and this must have helped him considerably to understand what one could and could not do with them. Having established the day on which the local weeklies went to press, he held weekly press conferences on the site at a time when the pressmen would be most likely to come. He briefed them carefully on the latest developments. It was a wise move. 'The Press,' as he wrote afterwards, 'is not always accurate and does not always emphasise those aspects of an excavation which are scientifically the most important; but sympathetic help from the directors of excavations is the best corrective of these failings, and may be regarded as a scientific no less than a social duty on the part of the modern archaeologist.'[11]

The results were of two kinds, the eye-catching short item and the more extended and sober report. There were plenty of examples of both. A photograph of a Chinese lady who, somewhat surprisingly, took an active part in the work at Maiden Castle one season, is headed: 'Studious Dorset Visitor from the Orient. Says Maiden Castle is "immense"', and underneath readers were told that the young lady in question came from Nanking and had spent three weeks digging at Maiden Castle.

The more detailed coverage would be of this kind:

Maiden Castle Excavations
Open to the Public for another Fortnight

The excavations at Maiden Castle have been delayed by the inclement weather and during the gale on Monday night tents were razed to the ground, necessitating the use by the campers for sleeping purposes of the hut which serves as an office.

Today Dr R. E. Mortimer Wheeler stated that the excavations would be open to the public for another fortnight. The latest finds include a number of glass beads elaborately decorated with spiral patterns in a well-known old Celtic style, while the Neolithic trenches at the east gate have produced axes of polished flint and other implements of the same material.

The east gate itself is now being rapidly cleared, and in two or three days' time it will be possible for visitors approaching from Winterborne Monkton to enter Maiden Castle actually on the surface of the prehistoric roadway. The post-holes of the gate structure are appearing rapidly and it will shortly be possible to reconstruct the town plan of the structure in one or two more of the prehistoric periods.[12]

This must be a fair summary of what Wheeler told the journalists at Maiden Castle. There are unlikely to have been more than three or four of them. The term 'press conference' was not used in the Thirties and it is really much too grand a term for what used to happen. One must forget any idea of dozens of journalists crowding eagerly round the sage and overwhelming him with questions. It was a small-scale affair, supplemented by the occasional specially arranged visit from the correspondent of *The Times*, *The Illustrated London News* or some equally serious publication, who had come down from London specially for the purpose.

But, before the Second World War, it was a wholly original idea to have regular press briefings on the progress of an excavation and there is no doubt that it achieved what Wheeler intended. Each week during the digging season the local press carried properly informed items about the progress of the dig and what was published there could, of course, always be picked up by the national papers, should anything especially newsworthy happen to be forthcoming. What Wheeler did, eagerly and quite deliberately, was to spread the concept of a dig being public property, something potentially

MAIDEN CASTLE, DORSET

Excavation of main rampart,
showing internal walling. Prehistoric oven in foreground.

33. *(above) and* 34. *(opposite). Two of the famous Maiden Castle postcards, a notable and profitable innovation on archaeological sites.*

MAIDEN CASTLE, DORSET

Floor of circular hut with chalk walls, 1st century B.C.

interesting to people who were not archaeologists. He used the Press, because that was the only medium available to him at the time. The BBC, in its radio days, was not interested, but after the war, when television had got going and a new breed of person was to be found in producers' offices, Wheeler grabbed at the opportunity with both hands.

We shall return to the matter of television in a moment, but meanwhile one should say something about Wheeler's other innovation at Maiden Castle, his campaign to attract visitors and to present the site to them in a systematic fashion. There were labels to indicate particularly interesting features of the work, skeletons were exposed to view in opened graves, students were appointed to act as guides and give lecturettes, postcards were printed – over 60,000 of them were sold on the site, together with many others in Dorchester – there were printed interim reports available at a shilling a copy – 16,000 of those were disposed of – and surplus small objects, such as sling stones and pieces of pottery, were on sale.

Wheeler himself had no doubts as to the wisdom of all this, but there were, inevitably, criticisms. Twenty years later he reminisced:

Our more conventional archaeological friends sometimes raised their eyebrows and sniffed a little plaintively at 'all this publicity of Wheeler's'. But we were not deterred and we were right, right not merely because this same public was incidentally contributing in gifts no small part of our considerable funds, but because I was, and am, convinced of the moral and academic necessity of sharing scientific work to the fullest possible extent with the man in the street and the man in the field. Today, in 1954, he is our employer. Today, ninety per cent of the money spent on field archaeology in Great Britain comes from our rates and taxes. This was not so in 1934; it might easily not be so now had we, and others like us, not deliberately built up a popular mood to which such expenditure was no longer wholly alien. It was not the least of our results at Maiden Castle that this mood of sympathy and half-understanding was by 1937 in the ascendant.[13]

This is perfectly true so far as it goes. Wheeler's great achievement as a publicist and public relations man for archaeology was certainly to persuade the public to agree to their rates and taxes being spent on archaeology, although the problem was rarely, if ever, expressed in quite this form. His definition of that mood as a combination of 'sympathy and half-understanding' is precisely right. It is just what television at its most successful can achieve and it is less, although no less desirable, than can be obtained from a reading of *Ur of the Chaldees*. Where the passage just quoted is misleading is Sir Mortimer's suggestion that, at Maiden Castle, he was handling 'considerable funds'. He was not, even if the money he spent is translated into its modern equivalent.

In 1936, an entirely typical year, the expenditure totalled £1,363, a sum within the same range as that for major excavations carried out before the First World War. Of this total, roughly £866 went on 'allowances and wages', £102 on photography and £46 on tools and equipment. The main items of income were £482 from sales and donations, £551 from private subscriptions and £288 from various societies. Not a penny was received from central or local government funds of any kind. The excavation was as privately funded as if it had taken place half a century earlier.

The work at Maiden Castle could, however, claim to have made some small contribution to the economy of the district, in the wages paid to workmen. These do not seem excessively high – £2 5s. 0d for a 45-hour week – but it was at a time of serious depression, when the agricultural wage had just been reduced from 31s. 6d to 30s a week, and for the 15s extra the Excavation Committee was paying one would have thought there would have been no problem in attracting an adequate number of reasonably satisfactory men. But, for some inexplicable reason, it was not so. Writing to Drew, his Co-Director, in 1937, Wheeler referred to the men they had employed the previous year as 'distressingly bad'. One wonders why. Was it, perhaps, because the men had to work harder at Maiden Castle than on farms? Or because unemployed men were afraid of being laughed at by their friends and acquaintances? Or, as a third possibility, because when times were hard, farmers and local councils kept only their best men and, possibly with some relief, put the others on the labour market?

A final comment on what one could call the human aspects of Maiden Castle might be concerned with the students who received part of their training there. They included a number who were later to occupy posts of distinction in the archaeological world. Mortimer Wheeler attached great importance to this aspect of the work. In 1921–22, when he was Keeper of Archaeology at the National Museum of Wales, he directed the excavation of the Roman fort at Segontium and it was there that he began to employ students as a matter of course, at a time when it was not at all normal to do so. There were, in any case, very few students to employ. Wheeler realised that there was a two-way advantage in having students on the site, the fact that they cost nothing in wages being incidental. On the one hand, the students gained valuable experience and made contacts which could be very useful to them in their careers, and on the other they helped to keep the Director in touch with new ideas and attitudes, a particularly important factor if the Director happened to be getting a little long in the tooth. Wheeler himself put the matter more delicately.

At Segontium, he said:

> . . . it became my mission – one which I have never since forsaken – to gather the younger generation about me in all my fieldwork, to inculcate it with controlled enthusiasm, and to give it in the formative stage a sense of direction, or at least of the *need* for direction. In return, these young people have served as a recurrent blood-transfusion into my own work.[14]

As a result of the 1939–45 War, the British archaeological tradition was considerably modified, to say the least, and in some ways broken. The middle classes no longer had the money or the leisure to which they had previously been accustomed; a different kind of educational system was in the making, with higher education much more easily available; it became accepted and normal that public money should be spent in ways that would have been considered impossible before the war; motoring was no longer thought of as the monopoly of the salaried classes; the members of the working class began to enjoy a level of security and comfort which made the Thirties seem like a bad dream. Archaeology had to adapt itself to this completely different social and economic environment, which was symbolised as well as shaped and assisted by the rapid growth of television.

This is not the place for a history of British television, but it is the moment to say something about what television did during the 1950s and 1960s to create what Sir Mortimer Wheeler so well described as 'a mood of sympathy and half-understanding' towards archaeology. This contribution centres around one particular producer, Paul Johnstone, who joined the BBC's

Television Service in October 1952, after the customary spell in radio, and remained with it until his much regretted death in 1976, having become in 1966 the first Director of its Archaeology and History Unit. Glyn Daniel, who worked much with him, later summarised his work on behalf of archaeology in these words: 'In a quarter of a century of television production he made an enormous contribution to establishing the name and nature and serious role of television, and made archaeology and history popular, interesting and absorbing'. This is not an exaggeration. Professor Daniel's assessment was confirmed in *The Times*' obituary, which said of *Animal, Vegetable, Mineral?*, and by implication of its producer, 'It was an instant and spectacular success. Libraries found that neglected shelves of archaeological books were suddenly empty.'[15]

Animal, Vegetable, Mineral? was a superior television quiz game, or, as Glyn Daniel called it, 'educated entertainment'. As we know now, but were less prepared to believe in 1952, there is apparently an insatiable public appetite for quiz programmes and anything which fits this recipe and possesses any merit and originality at all can hardly fail. In 1952, however, neither Sir Mortimer Wheeler nor Dr Glyn Daniel, the main performers, had any hopes at all of the new programme and only agreed to take part in it with considerable reluctance, which is one of broadcasting's major ironies.

The subjects to which Johnstone and the BBC's Archaeology and History Unit devoted themselves during the golden period which ended with Johnstone's death are far too numerous to list here, but a good selection of them is to be found in two books devoted to the Unit's productions, *Buried Treasure*,[16] written by Paul Johnstone himself in the mid-Fifties, and *Chronicle*,[17] edited by one of his colleagues, Ray Sutcliffe, as a memorial volume to him. They illustrate very well both the wide range of subjects which the BBC found suitable for television treatment and the kind of titles which were chosen in order to persuade the viewing public to watch the programmes.

Buried Treasure was a series of half-hour programmes broadcast in the early and mid-1950s. The programmes discussed by Johnstone in his book of the same name were: 'Piltdown Man' and 'The Alternative to Piltdown'; 'The Dawn of Art' (the Lascaux cave-paintings); 'The Walls of Jericho'; 'The Maltese Megaliths'; 'Stone Age House-building'; 'The West Kennet Long Barrow'; 'Stonehenge'; 'The Etruscans'; 'The Proud Princess' (an Iron Age royal burial at Vix, in eastern France); 'Maiden Castle'; 'The Peat Bog Murder Mystery' (the strangled body of a man found preserved in a peat bog at Tollund, in Denmark).

All these programmes were filmed on the original sites, so that each programme was something of a travel tale, and in every case the type of basic question to be answered was the same – 'What exactly are we looking at?'; 'What period in history does it relate to?'; 'What is the story behind it?'. The

35. *Piltdown Man, 1913. The Illustrated London News unknowingly popularises a magnificent fraud. The text below the picture reads: 'After the bringing to light of that remarkable "find" the jaw of the Sussex Man: Mr Charles Dawson and Dr A. Smith Woodward searching for other parts of the skeleton on the site of the first discovery.'*

producer took the most expert advice available, so that a considerable number of Europe's leading archaeologists became involved in the programmes and the scholarly base was unassailable. The presenters were Glyn Daniel and Sir Mortimer Wheeler, both of whom by now had become skilled performers in front of the cameras.

It is unreasonable to expect all things of all men, and what these *Buried Treasure* programmes consisted of was expertise applied at several different points. First, there was the imagination, judgement and organising ability of the producer, who was paid to know what the public could be persuaded to like and for his capacity to make superficially dull, forbidding or difficult material attractive and intelligible to ordinary people. Second, there were the technicians of many kinds who knew how to interpret the producer's wishes. Third, there were the acknowledged experts, the scholars, whose advice the BBC drew on in order to get the information right and who were paid a very respectable fee for their pains. And, fourth, there were the actual performers seen and heard in the programmes. By pooling the brains of all these people, it was possible, if all went well, to arrive at programmes which interested and pleased the public. No one person could possibly have fulfilled all these rôles, and everyone who was involved understood this perfectly well. Yet in a book or a magazine article, the author is expected not only to have a first class knowledge of his material but also to know exactly how to make it interesting to people he has never met and often cannot envisage. It is small wonder that so many so-called popular books and periodicals fail to be popular.

The second book connected with the name of Paul Johnstone, *Chronicle*, published eleven years later than *Buried Treasure*, illustrates how much further afield the producers were going in search of subjects by that time. Helped by much faster aeroplanes and bigger budgets, the world had indeed become their oyster. So there was 'The Return of the S.S. 'Great Britain'' (Falkland Islands); 'The Archaeology of the Boat' (Norway and North Germany); 'The Tutankhamun Post-Mortem' (Egypt); 'The Ashes of Atlantis' (The Aegean); 'Glozel' (France); 'The Lost Treasure of Jerusalem'; 'The Lost World of the Maya'; 'Islands out of time' (Easter Island); 'Maximillian' (Mexico).

During the latter part of the 1960s, a very fruitful partnership developed between Paul Johnstone's Unit and a young man on the way to making a great name for himself in television, Magnus Magnusson. Magnusson, born in Iceland and educated and living in Britain, had had an archaeological training and he became, in his very different way, televisions's successor to Sir Mortimer Wheeler. Essentially a populariser, in the Sir Leonard Woolley sense of the term, he is primarily a professional broadcaster and writer, not, as in the case of the *Animal, Vegetable, Mineral?* team, a professional archaeologist who took happily to broadcasting. In the last few years he has presented an important series, *The Archaeology of the Bible Lands*, with a book to accompany it; *The Vikings*, series and book, were equally prestigious, and he has been responsible for many individual archaeology programmes of high quality, in addition to being in charge of the extremely successful *Mastermind* series. He was a popular and unusually hard-working Rector of the University of Edinburgh and when, early in 1979, he gave a public lecture in York on the recent excavations in that city, the hall was packed and many failed to get in. It is difficult to see how any one person could have done more to carry on with Sir Mortimer's crusade to get the public interested in archaeology.

But the Council for British Archaeology is despondent. It believes that all the hard work that has gone into popularising and publicising archaeology has led nowhere. Before one tries to see if this tale of woe is really justified, it might be as well to let the CBA put its own case.

'The major problem of British archaeology still remains,' its Director, Henry Cleere, declared in the summer of 1979. 'It has so far failed to get its message over to the public at large. The success of archaeology on the media, attributable mainly to *Animal, Vegetable, Mineral?* and its successors in the 1950s and 1960s and the continuing growth of archaeology in the adult education field masks the fact that we have still not got properly over to the great mass of the population in this country the importance of a disciplined and logical approach to our heritage. The success of treasure-hunting, the quintessence of individualism and private enterprise, testifies to our failure. Our diehards retort that the only way to prevent pillage by treasure hunters is to invoke the full force of the law upon them. That is a course that must be explored, but it must be accompanied by a campaign of public education about the importance to us as a nation, collectively, of our heritage.

> The "media" are, by and large, not concerned with archaeology in its more mundane aspects, and only involve themselves when the sensational or the eccentric angles or a "story" suggest themselves. But this is not a phenomenon that is unique to the UK: most other countries have similar tales to tell. We still lack over here the ability to put over to the general public in an attractive way the excitement and challenges of archaeology. The crying need is for a truly "popular" magazine that can rival *Treasure Hunting* in its appeal. We have for long lacked magazines comparable *Archéologia* in France or *Archaeology* in the USA, which can be bought on station or airport bookstalls or studied in public libraries without elaborate preparations.[18]

How does one begin to discuss this, since what it is really complaining about is the sad fact that most of our fellow citizens are neither serious-minded nor well-educated, shortcoming which have been regularly lamented by those who are both of these things for two hundred years at least. Of

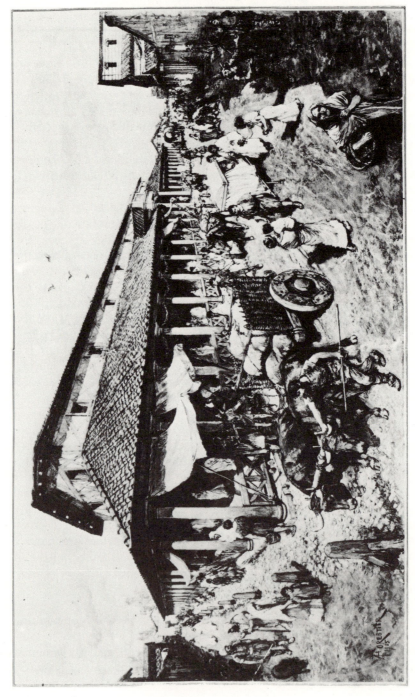

36. *1925. The Illustrated London News puts flesh on the archaeological bones. An artist's reconstruction of Viroconium, following recently completed excavations on the site.*

course it is regrettable that most of our fellow citizens do not have 'a disciplined and logical approach to our heritage', but, equally, they do not have such an approach to anything else. Generation after generation will go on trying to persuade children to set their sights just a little higher, but remarkably few of them do. When they become adults, they have much the same set of attitudes to life as their parents did. They prefer spending to saving and football to the ballet, the idea of good drinking and staying in bed on holiday in Jersey or the Costa Brava appeals to them infinitely more than a fortnight walking in the Highlands or visiting geysers in Iceland. They read the wrong papers, eat the wrong food, and keep their radios continuously tuned to the wrong stations. They believe in getting as much money as possible for as little work as possible and they persist, with untamable obstinacy, in believing that life is something to be enjoyed, preferably in the company of people very much like themselves. They are the despair of the thrifty, hard-working professional classes as much now as they have been for generations. They are, in other words, different and they have every intention of staying that way. They do not see life in terms of an examination, for which they are always preparing themselves, and they are rightly suspicious of anyone who seems to hold such a perverted theory. What appeals to them about archaeology is precisely what today's archaeologists go to such toffee-nosed trouble to decry, the treasure-hunting element, the pleasure of finding something exciting. They like mystery, murder, suspense and the successful detective, and Sir Leonard Woolley obligingly gave them all these things. Above all, they like archaeology to be *about* something, to have a good story in it, and, if that story is well told by a person they warm to, they will listen. There is nothing whatever surprising about this and there is something odd about people who think there is.

To whom, after all, does this somewhat elusive thing called 'our heritage' belong? The answer must be 'to everybody'. It is certainly not the monopoly of archaeologists, to be let out to other people only after a guarantee of good behaviour. Nobody should be allowed to blow up Stonehenge or Westminster Abbey, any more than they should feel free to demolish their neighbour's house or murder him, should such inclinations cross their minds, but to deny the attractions of treasure-hunting, with or without a metal detector, is to deny human nature. What is surely required is a much wider definition of treasure, not a scornful, wholesale rejection of the word. Henry Cleere is absolutely right in saying that the task is 'to put over to the general public in an attractive way the excitement and challenge of archaeology', but this can be done only by attractive and exciting people, who are in as short supply within the field of archaeology as anywhere else. With television cameras to help him, a likeable enthusiast can convince several million people that one little coin held the key to the whole history of a Roman site and that, had this coin never been found, for whatever reason, he would have had no story to

37. *Sir Mortimer Wheeler and Dr Glyn Daniel tasting, for the benefit of television viewers, the Iron Age gruel, which was prepared from a recipe reconstructed from an autopsy on the corpse of Tolland Man.*

tell.

What people resent is the idea that they are being asked or, even worse, ordered to change their habits and suppress their inclinations in order to make life easier or more profitable for some small sectional group. The British being what they are, nothing can ever come of a 'we know what's best for you' approach or of anything that looks like finger-wagging. The Puritan, whether of the academic or any other kind, is not a well-loved figure here. But, if it provides them with an enjoyable half-hour on television, which they rightly regard as existing primarily for entertainment and relaxation, archaeology, as Paul Johnstone realised, can win a lot of friends, which is what public relations is all about.

Against this background, one looks at the prospects facing our latest archaeological publication with more than usual interest. *Popular Archaeology* made its appearance in July 1979 and was an extraordinary commercial success from the start, which may not be altogether unconnected with the fact that its editor was Magnus Magnusson. The July issue, of which an optimistic 25,000 copies were printed, sold out in a few days, at a price of 65p, which many people in the trade would damn it from the beginning. Unlike *Antiquity*, it could be brought from newsagents and bookstalls in the ordinary way and it was printed in colour, with a cover that did not suggest a learned journal in the least. The people who bought it evidently liked what they were being given, because the second issue disappeared equally quickly.

The titles of the articles in the first two issues reflect the Editor's belief that interest begins at home. There is no attempt to follow Crawford's policy in *Antiquity* of covering the world in quarterly instalments. The main field is the British Isles, and in No 1 and No 2 we are offered, 'The Roman Sacred Spring in Bath'; 'Day out on Mendip'; 'Steam on the Road'; 'Cataloguing Cornwall'; 'Skarn Brae Revisited'; 'Day out in Offa's Dyke'; 'The Bigland Boat'; 'The Vikings at York'; 'The Experimental Iron Age Farm at Butser', and 'The Archaeology of Railway Stations'. We venture abroad only with 'Tigris', 'Santorini' and 'Chronicle – Filming the Maya'. There are practical features – 'Going on an Excavation'; 'Starting in Archaeology'; a 'Site of the Month' piece; a 'My Job' item – the subject of the first one was the Secretary of the Council for British Archaeology, Henry Cleere – a 'What's This?' section, and a round-up of news and topical controversies.

These were of course, early days, but certain deductions appear reasonable. The first and most important is that the magazine was not being bought only by libraries and people professionally concerned with archaeology. There were simply not enough of them to take 25,000 copies. The customers must have been the general public. The second thought that occurs to one is that the format, the style and the appearance of this new publication matched the title. It looked and felt like other hobby magazines and it suggested that it was not planned or published until reliable market research conclusions were available. And, thirdly, what readers were being offered for their 65p was good quality journalism, not slightly diluted learned articles. Both in print and on television, the editor was a well-informed specialist journalist, with a thorough understanding of his craft. Part of that craft is the ability to stimulate controversy and to get the paper talked about. With a sure touch, Magnus Magnusson chose metal-detectors and treasure-hunting, those twin bugbears of the Council for British Archaeology, as the subject for his leading article in the first issue. His aim, quite deliberately, was to provoke a reaction from as many people, in and out of the archaeological profession, as possible and in this way to get them involved in the venture from the start. It is a well-tried journalistic trick and, provided the subject is really in the air and ripe for discussion, it usually works. In this particular case it succeeded admirably. A very well-known public figure who obviously ought to have known better was apparently on the side of the treasure-hunters. Apoplexy occurred in the right quarters and *Popular Archaeology* had begun its career with a splendidly creative explosion.

This leading article is worth studying in detail. It is sensible, humane and written in a straightforward, conversational manner which produces no problems for the reader and makes him feel that he is among friends.

38. *Sir Mortimer Wheeler talks to Magnus Magnusson about his life and work in the first of two* Chronicle *films about him, broadcast by the BBC in 1972.*

Significantly, Magnusson uses the first person throughout, so proving that he exists and that he has opinions of his own. It would have been somewhat difficult for a television notability to pretend otherwise and, in any case, third person respectability is a doubtful merit in popular journalism.

The article is called 'The Perils of Treasure-Hunting', and reads as follows:

There is a Chief Steward on the British Airways Shuttle service between Glasgow and London (which I use with amazing regularity) who is a 'treasure-hunter'. That's to say, he owns a metal detector, and spends his off duty hours with friends and colleagues in a local society doing his bit of amateur archaeology.

He also collects Roman coins, and when we meet on the aircraft he usually has some new ones to show me that he has bought for his collection. He is immensely proud of his collection. It is helping to make him formidably knowledgeable about Roman Britain. And it gives his leisure hours real point and purpose.

And he totally and utterly condemns what he calls the 'cowboys' of metal-detecting who deliberately and ruthlessly pillage listed sites with their machines.

Metal detectors can obviously be a very real hazard to archaeological sites. But at the risk of offending purist friends and colleagues, I believe that metal-detector *users* can be of real benefit to archaeology – if their enthusiasm is harnessed and channelled into effectively supervised and systematically run local excavations.

'Treasure-hunting', whether you care to admit it or not, has been at the heart of all archaeology since the days of Heinrich Schliemann. However much we talk about distribution patterns and environmental services, every archaeologist secretly longs to make the great gold strike that will make his excavation famous. I argue that there is nothing to be ashamed of; what distinguishes the modern archaeologist is the control and discipline impressed on our digging. You cannot expect men to excise this fortune-hunting instinct. It is there. Whether it comes through the pools, or through sweeping a forbidden field, it is a factor in human nature that has to be reckoned with.

My personal belief is that 'archaeology proper', the profession of archaeology, should strive to welcome into the fold these enthusiasts with their metal detectors, to our mutual benefit. We have seen it happening in Industrial Archaeology, where the marvellous machines of the past have been given new life by the dedicated efforts of spare-time volunteers working to a disciplined schedule.

These men and women, working up to their oxters in mud and oil, helping to revitalise beautiful beam engines in the North, were first looked down on by the archaeological profession. Now they are accepted as an important element in the field of total archaeology and Kenneth Hudson would be the first to say so.

I feel that the same could apply to metal detectors and the treasure-hunting bug. If my Chief Steward on British Airways is a valid example (and I believe he is), we have in Britain a growing army of enthusiasts who are prepared to spend time and money on 'digging and delving' (my recreations).

I think it should be encouraged, and welcomed. Metal detectors are here to stay and it is plain silly to pretend they are not. Neither legislation nor 'approved codes of practice' will make them go away or lessen their potentially damaging effect.

I very much hope that metal-detector owners with a real enthusiasm for recovering the past (rather than winning the pools of the past) will co-operate through *Popular Archaeology* and their local societies in using their equipment, under supervision, towards the end to which we are all committed; an understanding of the past, rather than a rape of it.

It is a clever article, and the present writer is honoured, if a trifle surprised, to receive a mention in it. Very sensibly, it invites its readers to commit themselves to a cause, and, in the best manifesto tradition, it states plainly

39. *Paul Johnstone at Silbury.*

what that cause is, 'an understanding of the past, rather than a rape of it'. With that, not even the most rabid hater of metal-detectors could disagree; and, not surprisingly, it is exactly the same message as *The Antiquarian* had been preaching a century earlier. In fact, making allowance for the differences in social conventions, in journalistic style and in the nature of the intelligent reading public which have come about since the 1870s, there is a remarkable similarity between the aims and flavour of *The Antiquarian* and *Popular Archaeology*. If the two editors had been able to to talk to one another, a discussion which will have to await their eventual meeting in Heaven, they would have discovered that they had all the important things in common.

5 Amateurs and Professionals

Until the 1950s, most people who called themselves professional archaeologists would probably have said, as Sir Leonard Woolley and Sir Max Mallowan did, that they had blundered into archaeology in the first place. Fate simply turned their steps in that direction and a combination of luck, common sense and working with the right people allowed them to make a reasonable, sometimes a great success of the job. What happened to Dr Ralegh Radford,[1] now in his late seventies, is fairly typical of the interwar period.

Dr Radford took his degree at Oxford soon after the First World War. I was trained as a historian [he emphasises] and I was interested in architecture and I was also interested in the beginnings of the Middle Ages. My period of history is really post-Roman, say 400 to 1200, and historical sources in the conventional form – documents – are very scarce. It seemed to me that the one way of getting some further insight into the period was by archaeology, which meant, in effect, excavation. But I always regarded archaeology as a subject to be strictly controlled by the historical sources.

However, having decided that the sources for my particular period had to be supplemented by archaeology, I found myself in difficulties, because at that time there was no medieval archaeology. I am mainly interested in churches and it was quite clear to me that it wouldn't be sufficient just to dig and trace the lines of the masonry of vanished churches. One had to come to grips with the technical side of archaeology and the only way to do that was to go on a Roman excavation. These were the only ones in the 1920s that were being properly conducted. The excavation of prehistoric sites had hardly begun to get going then. So I went to Richborough. A. P. Bush-Fox, who was in charge there, was a friend of my father's. When he heard what I was trying to do, he said, 'Well, you'd better come to Richborough'. I didn't know Mortimer Wheeler in those days – he was the rising star, and most of the young people went to him – but I did know Bush-Fox. It was as simple as that.

Camping was always discouraged on these sites by people older than Wheeler and, anyway, I wasn't without financial resources, so I didn't need to camp. When I was away on a dig, I stayed either in a small hotel or in rooms. This was only for two or three weeks each year. But I soon realised that to get the kind of experience and information I needed I had to conduct an excavation on my own, and the first one I did was in Somerset, the Westland Roman Villa. Then, and afterwards, I got the men I wanted from a contractor, usually a road contractor. Usually one wanted a number of unskilled men – labourers, if you like – and a foreman to look after them. There was never any great difficulty in getting men in those days.

The way I told them what to do was this. I said they were to dig a certain trench four feet wide – it was marked out by stakes which the foreman drove into the ground under my direction. Usually one sank a test hole first and found that the Roman floor was covered by, say, three feet of debris. In that case I would say, "Dig to a depth of 2 ft. 9 ins.". It was the foreman's business to see that they dug to exactly this depth. I patrolled the trenches at intervals to make sure they weren't finding a standing wall, or something like that. The instructions were, "If you find a standing wall, stop work and send for the foreman". You always had to tell them exactly what you wanted done.

Like many other archaeologists, Ralegh Radford learnt all this the hard way. One made one's mistakes and tried not to repeat them. But he had firm ideas about the need to treat students and paid workmen in quite a different way.

Part of a student's training is to go on a dig. He gets board, lodging and pocket money. The workman gets a great deal more. If you are getting students to do your work, you are under an obligation to train them. You take them on that basis. Being the sort of photographer I was, I wouldn't have attempted to train a skilled photographer; but I had other students, at Glastonbury, for instance, who came there to learn the techniques of tracing robbed walls in the clay subsoil and similar things – how you got a register, why you registered depth in some cases and not in others, why it was no good recording to the nearest inch the depth of pieces of pottery in a foundation trench that was robbed in the early nineteenth century.

I always used contractors' men for the heavy work. I disapprove very strongly of using students for that, although I know it's almost universal today. I disapprove, because I say that under the modern system many of the students are not getting proper training. Students should not be used simply as muck-shifters. It's not efficient and it isn't moral.

When Ralegh Radford was learning his trade in the 1920s, it was considered abnormal, possibly eccentric or perverse, for an academic his-

40. *Small Down Camp, Evercreech, Somerset. Harold St. George Gray supervising the excavation of the Iron Age hill fort in 1912. The division between employer and employed is complete. The three labourers are paid to dig, while Mr Gray, who has thoughtfully provided himself with a deckchair, watches from above. The two boys are in an archaeological limbo, neither working nor supervising.*

torian to want to practise as an archaeologist. The best classical scholars and historians preferred to work on documents. That was the only way of making headway in one's profession. A doctorate was essential and, as Radford put it, 'you wouldn't have got a doctorate in those days for conducting an excavation unless you found something like a classical temple on the site.'

This attitude changed very quickly in the study of the Romano-British period, for the excellent reason that the amount of conventional documentary material available in this field was minimal. During the 1920s and 1930s, the archaeologists were building up the history of Roman Britain by uncovering what remained at such important sites as Richborough and Verulamium and doing their best to fill in the very sketchy outlines of what was already known from written sources. Even so, many of the details of this history are still the subject of great and occasionally passionate dispute.

Radford was and is what he describes himself as a Christian archaeologist, that is, someone whose prime concern is with the archaeology of churches and monasteries. 'Christianity,' he insists, 'was the hammer which beat out medieval society on the anvil of tribal society'. But, at the time when he needed it, there was no other archaeologist in Britain whose concern was with this particular period and aspect of history. There was only Mortimer Wheeler with his Romano-British sites, and, he estimates that something like 80 per cent of all the archaeologists of his generation in the interwar period were trained by Wheeler. The 20 per cent who gained their experience in other ways were all greatly influenced, through reading, discussion and visits, by Wheeler's methods and approach. There is a real point, therefore, in Wheeler's bon mot that no archaeologist in Britain was fit to be allowed loose on a site until he had the initials PRB – Passed Roman Britain – after his name.

The three giants of the Twenties and Thirties in Radford's view, the three people who pointed British archaeologists in the right direction, were Wheeler, O. G. S. Crawford and Graham Clark. Crawford, Radford believed, 'thought far more deeply and used a better philosophical background than Wheeler', and Clark was the great interpreter and visualiser of life in prehistoric times, with nothing but the archaeological and anthropological evidence to work from and with the vision to understand that he was dealing with the remains of living people.

It is very difficult to arrive at a reliable estimate of how many 'students' of archaeology there were at any given time during the 1920s and 1930s, if by 'students' one means people who were or who had been studying at universities and for whom archaeological experience was an important or essential part of their training for a future career. Conversations with a number of those who were responsible for excavations at this time suggest that in 1930 there may possibly have been fifty young men and women who fell within this category and in 1939, on the outbreak of war, possibly a hundred. To these would need to be added the handful of students from overseas, like Mortimer Wheeler's Japanese lady at Maiden Castle, who came to learn how the British did it.

These are probably slightly generous estimates, but the figures are in marked contrast to those to which we have had to become accustomed during the past twenty years. The Council for British Archaeology's comprehensive and useful *Guide to University Courses in Archaeology*, published in 1979, lists thirty-four British universities at which courses are offered with archaeology as the whole or part of the content of a first degree course. The importance and character of the archaeology in these courses varies greatly. In a number it is included as a relatively minor component of a course in classical studies; in others it is closely linked to studies in anthropology and in others again to geography or history. Not all courses include practical fieldwork, but many do.

Some undergraduate courses in archaeology, as for example those at Newcastle, are of a mainly cultural nature, but others are markedly scientific in their approach. At the School of Archaeological Sciences at Bradford, for example, the student is required to devote himself to 'computer appreciation; statistics; microscopy; photogrammetry and survey instruments; applied physics; the study of early technologies,' as well as to the full range of specifically archaeological techniques.

It would probably be a fair estimate to say that, in any given year since 1955, there have been between 600 and 1,000 students requiring practical site experience in archaeology as a necessary part of their course. Of these, possibly half, say 300–500, are contemplating archaeology as a full time career. If one adds to this a rather smaller number, perhaps 300, who, while not exactly students, are keenly interested and in many cases very experienced amateurs, one can easily see that a lot of sites are going to be needed each year to meet the demands of the people who want to dig, and that, looking at the matter from the point of view of the organisers, a great deal of intelligent and highly motivated voluntary labour is available. The way in which archaeology in Britain has developed since the Second World War has to be considered at least partly against this background.

One certainly need not assume that everyone who takes part in an archaeological excavation does so with a career in mind. For many people it is something that one learns to do for pure enjoyment, knowing that, as in the case of playing tennis or the piano, the more proficient one becomes, the greater one's pleasure is likely to be. A number of university extra-mural departments organise training courses to meet this particular need. In 1979, for instance, one could take one's pick of up to four weeks during July-August at Runcorn, Cheshire, on the site of a medieval priory and later mansion. 'Tuition,' said the advertisement, 'includes excavation techniques, finds processing, site draughtsmanship, and recording, practical work and lectures.[2] Both experienced and inexperienced diggers were welcome, at a cost of £7.50 a week. During the same summer, the University of Birmingham was offering a training excavation at Barnsley Park Roman Villa in Gloucestershire for 45 students, and special courses in archaeological surveying and drawing and in the identification of pottery and Romano-British artifacts.

Opportunities of this kind, with students paying a modest fee towards the cost of organisation and tuition, have been available each year since the early 1950s. A small proportion of those who take part arrive ill-equipped physically and temperamentally, with little real idea of what is expected of them, and for this reason the Council for British Archaeology has prepared a set of basic notes for new diggers. There is some practical advice on equipment.

Take old clothes for excavation, including some warm and waterproof garments for both on and off duty. If you are asked to provide your own trowel, this should be a mason's pointing trowel, blade 4 or 5 inches long, with a blade and tang drop-forged (riveted and welded trowels are not satisfactory for archaeological work). Even trowelling can produce blisters, so take some sticking plaster.

And there is further important information under the heading, *'Conduct'*.

It cannot be stressed too strongly that excavations are not organised vacations. Please remember always that the purpose of an archaeological excavation is scientific research and that all other considerations must be subordinated to this. Directors exercise absolute authority, and their instructions should be obeyed. Directors want their workers to enjoy themselves, and they usually do, but this is entirely secondary to the research work. Diligence, thoughtfulness, consideration of others, and good humour all help towards the success of an excavation. The work is often being undertaken under emergency conditions to salvage some record of the site before it is destroyed. The loss of even one pair of hands can make a difference to the results achieved, so please turn up if you have agreed to help. If you are simply looking for a holiday, think twice before applying.[3]

The paragraph just quoted is likely to be of considerable interest to future historians of archaeology in Britain, and probably to general social historians as well. The curiously puritanical-cum-military flavour is unmistakable – 'the Directors exercise absolute authority'; 'excavations are not organised vacations'; 'the purpose of an archaeological excavation is scientific research and all other considerations must be subordinated to this'; 'if you are simply looking for a holiday, think twice before applying'. What kind of people, one may well ask, need this sort of information? On what dreadful experiences is it based? Have Directors over the years been greatly plagued with people who apply, but never turn up, with lay-abouts who sit on the edge of the excavation enjoying the fresh air and the chance to acquire an agreeable tan, with undisciplined rebels who intend to go about the job in their own feckless way? Conversations with directors suggest that such things have indeed happened from time to time, but there seems to be no reason to believe that they are a frequent menace. The odd nuisance can be a severe trial, however, and anything that can be done to prevent him or her coming is no doubt a good thing, always remembering that one is dealing with people who have paid for the privilege of being members of the excavation's labour force. They are to that extent voluntary workers, and, as many non-archaeologists know all to well, volunteers for anything can present special problems of their own.

Even so, the repeated insistence on the serious purpose of the work on hand is surely a little disturbing. Why, one asks oneself, do all these

41. *Small Down Camp, Evercreech. With this part of the excavation completed, Harold St. George Gray, correctly dressed as a member of the archaeological officer class, stands thoughtful and victorious on the field of battle.*

enthusiasts want to come on a dig? If they have never been before, what do they imagine they are going to do there? The answer to the first question is that they come because television programmes and magazine articles have given them the idea that archaeology is a romantic business – which indeed it used to be –, that they might be able to do something useful – which is true –, and that, whatever the CBA may say, this is no bad way to spend a holiday and to meet like-minded people. Some of them, no doubt, have less of the driving demon in them than others and some are a trifle weak on scientific purpose, but most of them settle down well enough and not many digs are on the verge of mutiny all the time.

But – and there is an important but in all this –, why are professional archaeologists, the people whose income and career depends on the success of their excavations and surveys, so different from professional local historians? Why does archaeology, as a career, appear to attract people of an authoritarian temperament? One must not exaggerate this. It is certainly not true that all directors of excavations have Nazi tendencies, and it is important to remember in any case that, as we have said earlier, many excellent archaeologists, including some of the very best, have no wish to become involved in excavation. No harm is done either in mentioning, if not stressing, the fact that most site directors are well aware of the side on which their bread is buttered. They know that, with funds always short, they are usually dependent on volunteers in order to get any work accomplished at all and that it is in their own interests to create a pleasant atmosphere of the site. The majority of them achieve this without, apparently, any great difficulty. British archaeological sites may not be everyone's idea of a holiday camp, but they are certainly not slave camps either.

What one misses most, perhaps, is some more public recognition, expressed with greater warmth and friendliness, of the essential part which amateurs have played in the development of British archaeology during the past half-century and particularly since the end of the Second World War. Professor W. G. Hoskins, that great champion and helper of the amateur, has done this so well for local history that it seems useful to quote his words at this point, substituting 'archaeologist' for 'local historian' throughout. He wrote twenty years ago:

> We always do best those things we are not doing for money or that we are not obliged to do. The amateur – I hope it is clear that I am using the word in its original good sense – has made a large contribution to English local history in the past, and there is still plenty of room for him (or her) in this vast and still largely unexplored field. Indeed, it was amateurs who founded the study of local history and topography in this country, and who nourished it for four hundred years. One could truthfully say that the professional historian only entered this field when *The Victoria County History of the Counties of England* was founded in the year 1899. Even now, two generations later, the professional historian plays a very small part in the realm of English local history and topography, and this must always be so from the nature of the subject. There will be plenty of room for the amateur for centuries to come. He brings to the subject a zest and freshness, and a deep affection, which the overworked professional can rarely achieve. But he must also take his hobby seriously and go on enlarging his horizon and improving his technique to the end of his days.
>
> Primarily I regard the study of local history and topography as a hobby that gives a great deal of pleasure to a great number of people, and I think it wrong to make it intimidating, to warn them off because they may not have the training of the professional historian. It is a means of enjoyment and a way of enlarging one's consciousness of the external world, and even (I am sure) of the internal world. To acquire an abiding sense of the past, to live with it daily and to understand its values is no small thing in the world as we find it today. But the better informed and the more scrupulous the local historian is about the truth of past life, the more enjoyment he will get from his chosen hobby. Inaccurate information is not only false: it

is also boring and fundamentally unsatisfying. The local historian must strive to be as faithful to the truth as any other kind of historian, and it is well within his powers to be so.[4]

A careful study of this passage, with its delightful combination of amiability and sound advice, reveals a good deal of the predicament in which archaeologists find themselves nowadays. This predicament has two main causes – the attempt to make archaeology a science and the conviction that the work is desperately urgent, that, if it is not done today, the material on which it is based will probably have been destroyed or swept away by tomorrow. One might put this another way by saying that the local historian works under far less pressure than the archaeologist. Some part of this difference is due simply to style – more and more archaeologists in all countries like to be regarded as scientists, rather than as historians – but it is certainly true that in recent years archaeology has become more and more dependent on scientific and mathematical techniques and that anyone who has a career in archaeology in mind is virtually compelled to acquire at least a basic knowledge of what these techniques are and how they can be applied to his work. Broadly speaking, the more science a subject contains, the smaller the place there is in it for the amateur. Local history, as yet, makes very little use of science, in the strict sense of the term, so that it is always in a position to offer a welcome to the amateur who has nothing in his bag of tools but enthusiasm and a willingness to add to his knowledge and improve his methods. The humanities, one could say, find little difficulty in absorbing the amateur and making good use of his energy and talents; the sciences have a much greater problem with him, and tend to relegate him to relatively fringe tasks, of which one is digging and trowelling. It is this gradual movement towards a first and second team approach which has been mainly responsible for the unenviable position in which the professionals find themselves in Britain, needing the amateurs if the work is to be done at all, but mistrustful of them because they bring little to a site but common sense and a pair of hands. When this coalesces with daily fears of the disappearance of one's raw material, it is small wonder that the result has been a somewhat frantic atmosphere, in which the need for discipline and obeying the orders of the expert tends to be overemphasised. Any use of the word 'hobby' in such circumstances is likely to appear flippant and even heretical or obscene.

The way out of this frustrating state of affairs has already been innocently suggested by Professor Colin Renfrew, in a discussion called *The New Archaeology*, broadcast by the BBC, in 1972. What is meant by 'the new archaeology', he said, 'is a new approach to the prehistoric past which in many ways is more scientific not only because it uses scientific aids – radio-carbon dating and so forth – but chiefly because it is trying to set up rules of procedure for reconstructing the past and trying in that sense to be

42. *All-professional archaeology. Excavation of the Milk Street site in the City of London in 1977. No volunteers or amateurs are to be seen. All are professionals employed on contract.*

much more methodical than archaeology has been until now. One of the things archaeologists are insisting on now is that when we make a statement it shall be testable. We are trying much more deliberately to construct or invent theories about the past, and then go out and test them by excavation, rather than try to form an impression and subjectively paint a word picture.'[5]

More briefly, what this means is that Colin Renfrew is committing himself to the construction of archaeological models, which, whether one uses the word 'models' or not, is a normal and sensible way for any researcher in any field to proceed. But, more precisely, it indicates how the professional and the amateur can establish a fruitful partnership. The professional, the site director, will say, in effect: 'Here is the model of this particular aspect of life in the past which at the moment makes sense to me. On this site we have the opportunity to find out whether or not it needs modification. By working together here and by concentrating our attention especially on this or that, we should, with luck, be a little closer to the truth when we have finished and when the results of our common labours have been digested, analysed and interpreted than we were at the beginning. I will guarantee that, in exchange for all the work you are putting in, you will be kept properly and promptly informed as to what the end result is.'

This approach, which is already that of some of the most successful and imaginative site directors, avoids any temptation to use one's voluntary workers as coolies. It is a very natural human reaction to resent being 'used', to being no more than a stepping stone on someone else's path towards academic success and professional reputation, a mere pair of hands. There is no necessity for everyone working on a site to understand all the details of the laboratory techniques which may be used in the course of interpreting the finds – in all probability the director himself has only a fairly sketchy idea of what is involved – but what is essential is that everyone concerned shall be kept informed of what is going on and of the reasons for carrying out a particular task in a particular way. Even more important is the need to stay in touch with site helpers after the dig has been completed, in order to prevent the depressing feeling that one has been treated as expendable, that one's efforts have disappeared into some vast pit of scholarship and that one will never know what has become of them. All that is required is a brief handout, posted before too many months have elapsed, to tell the members of the team what the results of the excavation seem to have been. It is not sufficient, or courteous, simply to say, as the air hostesses do, goodbye and thank you.

In this respect, there is no real reason to discriminate between paid and unpaid workers, although one often hears the argument that the only duty a director has to an experienced excavator, hired on a short or long-term contract, is to give him reasonable working conditions and pay him. The difficulty is, of course, that there are now far too many experienced, trained archaeologists looking for jobs and in these circumstances certain traditions and courtesies may tend to be overlooked, on the basis of 'If you don't like my methods, you'd better find a job somewhere else', a somewhat unrealistic piece of advice when one considers the state of the labour market for this particular expertise. The story is told of the girl employed by the London Excavation Unit to work on sites within the City boundary. Paid, like her colleagues, the miserable salary of between £2,500 and £3,000 a year, she received a summons to her bank manager to explain why her account was overdrawn and what she proposed to do about it. 'You're a graduate, said the manager, 'what are you doing with the other half of your salary? Why isn't it being paid into your account?' 'There is,' she told the unbelieving manager, 'no other half of my salary. This is it, all of it.'

What one sees in present-day British archaeology is, in fact, the fairly brutal operation of the Victorian economic theory of supply and demand. There are far too many archaeologists chasing too few jobs, wages are depressed in consequence, and, not unnaturally, one comes across young professionals or would-be professionals who object strongly to the practice of employing volunteer unpaid labour, which, in their view, reduces their chances of employment even further. There is no solution to this problem, so long as an unrealistic number of graduates continues to pour out of the archaeology departments of our universities each year, and so long as the amount of public and private money invested in archaeology remains at its present level. One cannot blame project directors for using volunteers, if the alternative is to have no excavation at all, and one can hardly expect an organiser to pay £5,000 a year, if he knows he can get people for £2,500, particularly under conditions of great urgency, when what is an exciting hole in the ground today is going to be a large office block or a hotel in two years' time.

It needs to be recognised, however, that the highly competitive labour situation in archaeology has to a considerable extent conditioned the kind of person who is likely to succeed. The thrusting, tough, often ruthless type is the one who gets and holds the job and achieves promotion. When both money and time are short, it is important to acquire the reputation of getting things done, no matter what the conditions are. This is another way of saying that during the past thirty years, managerial skills have become increasingly important. Yet, strangely enough, none of the departments of archaeology in British universities appears from its syllabus to make any deliberate attempt to teach these skills, although no doubt students are encouraged in an informal and incidental way to develop them. What should surely have become normal practice by now is to include in every archaeological degree or diploma course what is provided by the Department of History and Archaeology at the Dorset Institute of Higher Education as part of the course for its Certificate in Practical Archaeology, under the heading 'Professional Studies'. here the student is required to acquire a satisfactory knowledge of 'the philosophy and history of archaeology; the structure of British archaeology; administration and management in archaeology; the structure of local government; archaeology and planning', and one cannot help feeling that he or she will be all the better for it.

There is, however, another aspect of archaeological training which merits discussion. It is certainly true, as we have said earlier, that archaeology is not simply a matter of excavation, and it is equally true that a high proportion of archaeology graduates will never earn a living, or want to, from the practice of archaeology. For these two reasons alone, any undergraduate course in archaeology or involving archaeology must be of general educational value. It must be broadly based and it must not aim at producing people who are primarily technologists, whatever the nature of the available archaeological jobs may turn out to be. What must be done, nevertheless, and what is being done only in the most desultory way at the moment, is to take care to select, as part of one's annual student intake, people who have the temperamental qualities which will allow them to become successful archaeological managers. Personal observation suggests that many, if not most of today's younger site organisers and supervisors could have had a very rewarding career in industry, particularly in those branches of industry, such as mining, petroleum or construction, where adaptability to constantly changing conditions is a prime requirement. They are not necessarily very nice people, but that, as industry and commerce know very well, often goes with the breed.

On big excavation projects, some division of function is inevitable. In industrial terms, the director then becomes the general manager and each main area will have its own production manager, who is responsible for day-to-day progress. There will also be people who specialise in welfare, catering and the other forms of expertise which any major industrial activity requires. Many archaeologists, experienced or not, find this form of organisation unpleasant, and do their best to keep away from it, just as many people have no wish to work in a large factory or a large office organisation. One of the great attractions of British archaeology during the post-war period has been that it could always be relied on, season after season, to provide a good mix of sites, some small and friendly, where the director is around all the time and where conversations are on equal terms, and others which recall an Army camp before the Normandy landings, where everyone has his own job to do, where orders and information moves downwards through a carefully organised and clearly understood chain of command and where the commanding officer appears only rarely, to satisfy himself that all is well and to address the troops from time to time, when their level of morale seems to demand it.

One could usefully study a selection of recent excavations from this point of view, looking particularly at the number and kind of people involved, the balance between amateur and professional workers and sources of finance and local help. It might be useful to begin with a large and prestigious excavation, of the full modern type. The one carried out by Leslie Alcock at South Cadbury Castle in Somerset would do very well.

After preliminary excavations in 1966, work began in earnest the following year. Excavations lasted for seven weeks during July and August and continued until 1969. About 250 people took part each year, many of them, as Alcock gratefully acknowledged, 'entirely at their own expense'.[6] This does not mean, of course, that whenever one visited the site one would have seen 250 people digging there. The diggers came and went, some spending a fortnight there, some more. But, this notwithstanding, it was a large affair and, because it was large, it had to be well organised. The carefully structured nature of the army commanded by Professor Alcock was made clear by the use of different colour of the hard-hats worn by the various grades of excavator, with a special colour reserved for the director himself. How much this benefited discipline and morale is difficult to say, but there is some evidence that most of those directly concerned found the system a rather agreeable military joke.

The cost each year was about £5,000, which means roughly £10,000 at today's prices. It was kept at this very modest level only as a result of the great amount of unpaid work that was put in by a wide range of people. These included not only the volunteer excavators, but Kodak, which looked after the photography and the 30th Signal Regiment, which provided and manned field telephones. The romantic nature of the site, supposedly King Arthur's Camelot, undoubtedly helped and the largely mythical association with the mainly legendary King Arthur was fully exploited for fund-raising purposes, both in Britain and in the United States.

The Camelot Research Committee, as it very wisely called itself, raised its £5,000 a year partly by individual donations and partly by the sale of offprints and postcards on the site, in the best Wheeler and medieval pilgrims tradition, but chiefly by grants from societies and institutions. One or two of these were local – the Somerset Archaeological Society and Morlands Charitable Trust –, others, like the Honourable Society of the Knights of the Round Table, were persuaded to subscribe because of the well-publicised link with King Arthur, and others again – the BBC, TWW, and the *Observer* – because they were in the field of popular history and legend. But the bulk of the support came from the same bodies that had made the work at Maiden Castle possible, the British Academy, the Society of Antiquaries, universities and colleges.

What has to be stressed here, however, is that without amateur help Leslie Alcock would have been hard pressed to find the money to carry out the work on the scale he felt the site demanded. It would probably be no exaggeration to say that the unpaid labour he attracted was worth £2,000 a year to him, a consideration of some consequence.[7]

43. *Feminism and archaeology. A majority of today's archaeology graduates are women, a point well made in this picture of the Milk Street site in the City of London in 1977. Three of the four people working on the mosaic are women.*

At the same time, Professor Barry Cunliffe was concluding his work at Fishbourne, where the Roman-British palace was to prove to be the greatest archaeological tourist mecca so far seen in Britain, with a quarter of a million visitors during the first six months after the site and its museum were opened to the public. The digging season at Fishbourne was shorter than at Cadbury, lasting for about five weeks, but, over a period of seven years, 60 volunteers a day were at work there. There could have been many more, but Professor Cunliffe decided to hold the numbers at this figure. The professional element in the excavation was very small. The arrangements for the final season in 1967 were typical.

The excavation was sponsored by the Chichester Civic Society and financed by grants received from the British Academy, the Ministry of Public Building and Works, the Society of Antiquaries, Chichester Corporation, the Adorian Archaeological and Educational Trust, and the Sussex Archaeological Society. Mrs Cunliffe took charge of the finds and pottery, Mr David Baker was the site photographer, and Mrs Margaret Rule undertook the general supervision, including the conservation work, before and after the main period of excavation. During the summer period, the actual excavation was under the day-to-day supervision of four people, N. J. Sunter, B. M. Morley, P. Green and the Rev. A. B. Norton. it was, not to labour the point unduly, yet another excavation which would never have happened if an ample supply of volunteer workers had not been available.

The same pattern has repeated itself over and over again. At Portchester Castle in the late 1960s and early 1970s, Professor Cunliffe achieved excellent results by using a floating labour force of between 30 and 40 student volunteers each day, with adequate, but by no means generous expert supervision throughout. At Winchester, as we have already mentioned above, the great Martin Biddle's excavations found useful work for about 170 people every day, most of them volunteers. At Dragonby, in Lincolnshire, Jeffrey May worked somewhat differently during the excavations he carried out on the site of an Iron Age fort between 1964 and 1969. Although in the actual excavation work he had the help of a number of people termed, perhaps euphemistically in some instances, 'students', his main use of genuine students was in a specialist capacity, and supporters of the feminist cause will take pleasure in noting that a high proportion of them were women. There were six men and one woman as field supervisors; a surveyor, male; five women engaged in recording, and three women and one man in conservation work; one palaeobotanist, a man; and three catering people, all women.

A substantial part of the help Mr May received was not on the site at all. He acknowledged as especially valuable the services of the following:

Messrs. A. Wright and M. Howlett, for greatly valued facilities at the

Central Research Laboratory at the Normanby Park Steel Works; Mr. M. Parkes and Mr. M. Simms, of the Ore Mining Branch, for the loan of machinery for stripping topsoil; the Lindsey Education Committee for the renting of Dragonby School at a nominal rate; to Shell Chemicals for the gift of polyethylene glucol; to R. T. B. Redbourne Works and the Norman Park Works Canteen for catering; to Mr. H. Rusling for the loan of houses at Bagmoor Farm.[8]

Details like this are a reminder on the one hand of the remarkable variety of ways in which an important archaeological project can strike roots in the local community and on the other of the very unsatisfactory nature of the word 'amateur'. Jeffrey May received invaluable help from people with no form of expertise as archaeologists, but whose specialist skills as metallurgists, mining engineers, chemical engineers and caterers made it possible for the excavation to function and to obtain useful results. In the same way, to classify 20 or 50 field workers simply as 'amateurs', 'students' or 'volunteers' can be extremely misleading. It may perhaps look better in a report if one's volunteer workers are described as students, although this can sometimes flatter the persons concerned and, on the other hand, someone who decides to spend a week or two of his holiday in this way may well be a chemist, botanist, engineer or architect, with specialist skills which may be of use to the director.

Whatever criticisms of detail one may choose to make, the indisputable fact remains that during the post-war period the British have achieved something remarkable in harnessing the energy and enthusiasm of many hundreds of amateur archaeologists and in making it possible for them to work happily and usefully with a relatively small number of professionals. As we have suggested earlier, if one could have taken a God's eye view of Europe at any time in July, August or September between, say, 1950 and 1980, one would have observed quite a different pattern of archaeological activity in England and Wales compared with the Continent. On the Continent, East and West of the Iron Curtain, one would have found a very small number of excavations in progress in each country, well-financed from official funds and for the most part tightly controlled by the appropriate Ministry or by some major State museum. In Britain, on the other hand, one would notice a generous scatter of sites, usually quite small and nearly always underfinanced, made possible only by the joint efforts of professionals and amateurs, working on what would be considered abroad as a dangerously loose rein. Our heavenly observer would probably feel inclined to make three further comments – that the British method produced a greater bulk of scientific information each year, that it created a considerable body of people trained in archaeological techniques and that, linked with exceptionally good television coverage, it was very helpful in bringing about an enligh-

44. *The archaeological labour force in 1979. The GPO site in the City of London. Nearly every member of this group is a paid, graduate professional. All are under 30 and most under 25. Older people, with family responsibilities, could not exist on the wage offered. They are wearing the modern archaeologist's normal summer outfit. The site-supervisor here has a small army under his control.*

tened public opinion where archaeology was concerned. He would come to the conclusion, on reflection, that archaeology in Britain was a haphazard, pragmatic and democratic affair which, like so many British institutions, somehow worked.

It is normal in Britain for private individuals and organisations to get an activity launched and to nurse it through its early stages and then, once its worth and need have been proved, to persuade the Government to take it over and to provide finance on a scale which only the public purse can make available. One has seen this in a number of fields – hospitals, the support of the poor, aged and unemployed, education and libraries are a few of them – and the gradual movement of the State into archaeology was inevitable, although it has proceeded far too slowly and parsimoniously for many people's satisfaction.

The key year from this point of view will probably be seen by future historians to have been 1971, when the Department of the Environment was set up. The former Ministries of Public Building and Works, Housing and Local Government, and Transport disappeared, and the work of the new Department was made the responsibility of three Ministers. The Minister for Housing and Construction now looked after, among other matters, ancient monuments, housing programmes and general environmental improvements. The Minister for Local Government and Development was given charge of roads, the countryside and conservation, local government and transport planning. The Minister for Transport Industries was concerned with railways, inland waterways, ports and general policy on the nationalised transport industries. This still left ancient monuments as the business of one Ministry and conservation as that of another, but the grouping of roads, historic buildings and conservation within a single Government Department was, at least potentially, of great value, since it could help to prevent the clash of interests which had happened so often in the past, when it often appeared that proposals for new roads were considered far more important than any historical, architectural or archaeological considerations. Whether the situation has in fact improved a great deal is a matter for some dispute. The construction of new roads has recently been brought almost to a standstill as a result of the nation's serious economic position, but until 1978 at least it had an overall priority which tended to make short work of historical relics.

It so happened, however, that *Rescue*, one of the most important developments in British archaeology during the present century, was established in the same year as the Department of the Environment. It is a peculiarly British institution, which once again made it possible for individuals and independent bodies to carry out work which no official body was undertaking and may possibly be another stepping stone towards a State Antiquities Service.

The Council for British Archaeology was established in 1944, with a mainly institutional membership, although there are some individual sub-scribers. It exists to provide an information service for its members, to formulate and present a general policy on behalf of archaeology and, in every way possible, to act as a pressure group. Its funds come mostly from its members, but it receives a small State grant. It is not allowed to finance excavation work.

Broadly speaking, *Rescue* was founded to carry out the work which the State was not doing and which the CBA was not permitted to do. The annual loss of sites was 'accelerating beyond the ability of archaeologists either to excavate or record them. Many of the threatened areas cannot even be surveyed before they are obliterated.'[9] In order to deal with this situation, the CBA continued to press for a properly funded State Antiquities Service, which would work through regional centres and which would be able to deal with emergency situations well in advance, through consultations with planners and developers. Since it was obvious, however, that such a development was most unlikely to take place in the near future, what became known as *Rescue* was created.

> *Rescue* was defined as an association of *all* interested people, with individual membership; and a fund-raising body, obtaining funds from subscriptions, donations, etc. *Rescue* aims to use its resources in general to help to record and conserve the physical remains of the archaeological heritage, and specifically to support surveys, to acquire sites or areas of archaeological importance for permanent conservation, to initiate and support rescue excavations and the publication of their results.[10]

Rescue moved very quickly into action, with a leaflet campaign, a travelling exhibition, and the appointment by local societies of liaison officers responsible for channelling information from *Rescue* to the Society and of Regional Officers with the task of publicising the aims of *Rescue* within their regions. Everyone who has been in any way connected with it agrees that the creation of *Rescue* was of immense significance, but there seems to be some degree of controversy as to exactly why it was significant. There are those who put the main emphasis on the amount of information gathered from the high-speed emergency digs which were carried out with the help of the new organisation, others who find the greatest value in the new sense of urgency which *Rescue* was able to bring to the whole situation of archaeology in Britain, and others again who viewed *Rescue* with special favour, because it seemed to put the non-excavating archaeologists firmly where they belonged, in second place, and to turn a bright spotlight on the profession's heroic shock troops, the diggers, for whom no task was too arduous, no peril too great. The wisest judgement, however, is probably that of Professor Charles Thomas, who felt that *Rescue*'s most remarkable achievement was to have forced well-established, highly respectable ar-

45. *The modern professional's foul-weather kit. Women on the Bayard's Castle site in the City of London in 1975. Hard hats are being worn because this is a building site and the archaeologists are required to conform to contractors' regulations.*

chaeologists into political action, or, as he admirably put it, into 'heavy involvement with the unfamiliar and slightly shark-infested world of the mass-media and the public relations industry'.[11] It was, he was sure, something quite different from 'that sorry process, the splintering off from an old, or old-middle-aged, County archaeological society by younger activists, fed up with brass-rubbing, mosses, picturesque ruins, or any of the modern equivalents, and eager to engage in dirt archaeology, often under ludicrously incapable direction, and – as often – with numbers and resources insufficient to support the appropriate publication of results.'[12]

This may well be so, but there is a fallacy here, not so much in Professor Thomas's argument, as in that of the people who equate physical activity with virtue. There is no doubt that one major reason for the great appeal which excavation has for the young is that it involves using one's muscles. There is earth to be shifted and exposure to the hazards of the English climate and pioneering living and sleeping conditions in tents and church halls, compared with which challenges and delights the study of old churches and ruined castles has little to offer. The argument is a foolish one, but it is effective and widespread, and in this sense one could say that *Rescue* has been a bad influence, since it helped to encourage the unhelpful but fashionable belief that archaeological salvation was to be obtained only through digging.

The decline in prestige of church archaeology is particularly to be regretted, since Britain's churches, ruined and intact, are such a splendid historical laboratory, covering so many centuries. This state of affairs is probably caused in part by the steady fading away of that great stalwart of Victorian and Edwardian archaeology, the scholarly parson. In April 1973, a conference on *The Archaeology of Churches* was held at the University of East Anglia. it was organised jointly by the Council for British Archaeology and the Board of Extra-Mural Studies of the University of Cambridge, 'to draw the attention of not only archaeologists, but also planners and others responsible for churches to the amount of historical information which can be derived from an investigation of both their fabric and site,'[13] a fact which was perfectly well known a century ago, but which today needs to be presented by means of a conference to a generation which has been dazzled by decades of well-publicised excavations. The most significant feature of this particular conference, however, was not that the archaeologists, historians and planners came, but that the clergy, of all grades and kinds, stayed away.

What one reads in the Annual Reports of the Council for British Archaeology is not necessarily representative of the opinion and morale of archaeologists as a whole, since, as we have already pointed out, the CBA is essentially a body reflecting the views of institutions and of those who earn their living from archaeology. The large number of amateurs and fringe operators who devote much of their spare time to archaeology may well see the current situation quite differently. What Equity thinks and does is a poor guide to the opinions of the members of Braitin's innumerable amateur dramatic societies and our amateur music-makers and concertgoers live in quite a different world from the professionals who try to defend their interests by belonging to the Musicians' Union. But, even so, the changes which occur in the viewpoint and obsessions of the CBA from year to year must be based on some kind of reality, on some modifications of the national context within which archaeolgists of all kinds have to work. The CBA Reports represent one type of official view and, being for that reason political documents, they need to be read and interpreted with some care. This being so, the shift of emphasis over the past few years must have some significance. It must indicate a trend of some kind, a new order of priorities.

In 1976 the CBA informed us that the picture was a very gloomy one. The previous year had been 'dominated by the economic crisis'. There had been 'a perceptible decrease in the amount of excavation carried out during the year', archaeologists were finding fewer and fewer opportunities of employment, less money for research was available at universities and elsewhere, museums were being forced to cut their budgets. About the only encouraging feature of the situation was that the activities of property developers and motorway builders had slowed down, so that one kind of pressure on archaeologists had been eased.

By the following year it appeared that there was some advantage in being poor. The CBA observed with approval, 'the increasing involvement of non-professional archaeologists in the work of professionals' and went on to say:

> A disquieting polarization between professionals and amateurs had been observable in British archaeology in recent years. The financial stringencies of the present time may well have made the professionals aware that local groups represented a considerable resource that they would disregard only to the detriment of their own work, and so the non-professionals are now being assimilated into the overall structure for British archaeology that is painfully beginning to evolve.[14]

This might perhaps have been better put. Not many of us are likely to relish the thought of being assimilated into a structure, and only those with an exaggerated respect for organisation would wish to see the situation develop in quite this way. Being 'assimilated into a structure' sounds uncommonly like being a cog in a machine, and that, surely, is not an agreeable thought.

But after a little reflection one sees what the CBA means. The grand old days of dig-where-you-like are disappearing as fast and as surely as economic laissez-faire has done but, while they lasted, it was good to be alive. It is, however, possible that those recalcitrants who fail to thrill to the idea of an

46. *L'Ancresse Common, Guernsey, 1979. The excavation of this Neolithic chambered tomb was sponsored by La Société Guernesiaise and directed by Dr I. A. Kinnes, of the British Museum. The workers were all volunteers and, as the photograph shows, of various ages. This was a typical example of the British recipe for amateur–professional co-operation.*

all-embracing structure, neat and tidy organisation and well-disciplined activity may be turning to metal-detectors as an outlet for their individualism. One reason, perhaps the chief one, why professional archaeologists hate metal-detectors so much is that they see them as symbols of a refusal to be organised, of the free enterprise operator who, a century and a half ago, would have enjoyed himself digging up barrows to see if there was anything interesting inside. The new race of maritime of marine archaeologists appears to feel just the same about the amateur divers who locate and explore wrecks with gold rather than science in mind. The trouble is, of course, that the professionals have found too much treasure themselves in the past. From an archaeological point of view, the curse of Tutankhamun has been not that people connected with that particular excavation have come to a sudden and occasionally unpleasant end, but that the discoveries of such a great quantity of gold and jewellery were so exciting to the man in the street, who was only waiting for the arrival of the cheap metal-detector in order to, as he felt, ape his betters and to have a go himself. Metal-detectors are disturbingly democratic.

To the organisation-minded person, there is undoubtedly something very attractive and satisfying about the concept of a comprehensive State archaeology system, and there are indeed considerable advantages in such an arrangement – a well-defined career structure, security of employment, simplicity of negotiation over funds, easy contacts at Ministerial level, are some of the most obvious. But there are real disadvantages as well, as acquaintance with Continental methods soon reveals. The British approach so far – it would be unfair to call it a system – has produced considerable frustration in some quarters and no doubt a certain amount of wastefulness and inefficiency, although inefficiency is very difficult to assess, but it has deep roots and it has allowed a remarkably wide range of people to develop an understanding of what archaeology is about and to make a valuable contribution to its development. To make radical changes in the interests of a thoroughgoing, fully State-funded system would be very foolish, especially at the moment, when the peculiarly British mix of amateur-professional workers and private-public finance has been producing such excellent results.

We do in fact appear to be moving towards the right answer, with *Rescue* on the one hand and the Department of the Environment's Central Excavation Unit on the other. The Unit was set up in 1975, with an interesting brief. Its work falls into two parts. It has special and continuing responsibilities towards the archaeology of the Roman frontier in northern England and for work carried out at Royal palaces and public buildings in London, and it is equipped to carry out a flexible programme of excavations in places where other organisations lack the necessary resources. The Unit can operate entirely independently, or in collaboration with local societies or groups, or on projects which need extra staff or specialist advice. Centres for report writing and storage have been set up at Portsmouth and Carlisle, with a standard recording system for all excavations in which the Unit is involved.

The reporting and recording elements in the organisation of the Central Excavation Unit are particularly important, because it is in precisely these aspects of archaeological work that there has been the greatest weakness during the post-war period. One could perhaps describe the malady as excavation constipation, a serious complaint, in which far more information is taken into the system than can possibly be processed and digested. Every year the mountain of notes and records gets bigger, publication falls further and further behind, and access to what the excavators have discovered becomes more and more difficult. In many ways, a total ban on excavation for five years would be a great blessing, but that, alas, is hardly practicable. The fact remains that the whole point of archaeology, as of any other form of scholarship, is to make new information available to those who would like to make use of it and that, under present conditions, is happening only in an erratic and unreliable fashion.

Something has clearly gone wrong, and the Director of Bristol City Museum, Nicholas Thomas, himself an archaeologist of considerable standing, has no doubt as to what it is. In his Presidential Address to the Council for British Archaeology, delivered on 16 July 1976, he chose as his text, 'that the almost complete separation of units and other organisations for rescue digging from museums is a disaster for British archaeology'.[15] Explaining why he felt this to be so, Mr Thomas reminded his audience that a dig was useless without what he called 'the archive', and he went on to define 'archive'. 'An archive,' he said, 'is the full product of a dig, from start to finish, everything from letters about ownership of hypothetical finds, through the artifacts, the scientific samples, the plans, sections, and complete documentary side. But it is more than that, it is also the information already existing, together with the finds that may already be in the museum's stores or on show.'[16]

Ideally, this is certainly true. To have the whole archive in one place, to be able to get the whole story without moving from the building, is any researcher's idea of Paradise. How often can it be achieved is another matter, but Nicholas Thomas is right in saying that a museum is the only real possibility. Nowhere else, except in one's own home or office, can one have artifacts and documents together, and this, of course, is exactly what many nineteenth-century archaeologists contrived to do.

Under today's conditions, when the mass of material to be brought together for recording and study is so large, the creation of an archive, in the sense in which Nicholas Thomas uses the word, has to be a professional job. Amateurs may and do provide much of the material that finds its way into the archive, but its actual preparation demands special skill and experience. A good deal of the routine work, even so, can be carried out by inexperienced

47. *Employer and employed together in the same hole at the Sanctuary, Wiltshire, in 1930. Lt. Col. Cunnington, in charge of the excavation, is distinguished by wearing a jacket and hat; the hired workman, by contrast, is seen in shirtsleeves and a cap.*

people, under skilled direction. At Bristol, for instance, Job Creation employees have been used with great success in this way and there is no reason why much of this type of processing work should not eventually be done by volunteers. It may not have the same glamour about it as excavation or the same outdoor joie-de-vivre, but there is no doubt at all that we have reached the stage at which without a vastly increased processing of finds – recording, indexing, conservation, publication – a great deal of excavation is likely to be a waste of time and precious resources. We have only just begun to work out what an acceptable and fruitful blend of amateurs and professionals might mean on the indoor side of archaeology, after nearly half a century of experiments outside.

In saying this, one is not thinking only of excavation. Recording buildings, conducting surveys of town areas and recording graveyards are equally urgent and valuable archaeological pursuits, and the results of such work have to be processed and stored in exactly the same way as discoveries from an Iron Age fort. The amateur-professional partnership is essential from one end of the archaeological spectrum to the other.

It would be interesting to know, incidentally, how many holders of British passports have entered the word 'archaeologist' as their occupation. And how many have put 'archaeologist' on a Census form. If we could discover these totals – and there seems to be no good reason why the authorities should refuse to co-operate – we might get some reliable idea at least as to how many people in Britain consider themselves to be professional archaeologists. What proportion by any reasonably objective standard actually are would, of course, be another matter.

6   The Industrial Archaeologists

The term 'industrial archaeology' seems to have been invented at some time in the early 1950s, probably by Donald Dudley, who at that time was Director of Extra-Mural Studies in the University of Birmingham and who later went on to become Professor of Latin in the same University. Mr Dudley had become interested in archaeology through his classical studies and it was no doubt the beauties of nineteenth-century Birmingham and the Black Country, somewhat battered by wartime bombing, which made him feel that industry was as entitled as any other form of human activity to its archaeology. One of his colleagues, Michael Rix, offered the idea to the world in an article which he wrote in 1955 for *The Amateur Historian*, defining the scope of the subject as 'the steam-engines and locomotives that made possible the provision of power, the first metal-framed buildings, cast-iron aqueducts and bridges, the pioneering attempts at railways, locks and canals'. All these, together with factories, mills and workers' housing, represented, he believed, 'a fascinating, interlocking field of study, whole tracts of which are virtually unexplored'.

It is interesting to note that neither of the begetters of industrial archaeology had any first-hand experience of engineering, industry or technology. Mr Dudley was a classicist and Mr Rix an architectural historian. Both, in fact, were humanists, and it was significant, in view of subsequent developments, that the subject should have originated in the first place as a branch of the humanities, that is, as a study primarily concerned with people, not with things. The history of technology, of which the Newcomen Society had been the major impresario since the 1920s, had exactly the opposite emphasis. Its raw material consisted of machines, techniques and processes.[1] It had much to say about inventors, but the people who operated the machines and learned the techniques were incidental to the main study and were rarely mentioned.

The first conference on industrial archaeology, or rather, industrial monuments, was organised by the Council for British Archaeology in 1959, and the first book on the subject,[2] published in 1963, was inspired by that conference and drew its shape and its ideas from it. A quarterly *Journal of Industrial Archaeology* was launched in the following year and by that time industrial archaeology had begun to recruit its army of supporters and activists, remarkable both for their numbers and for their variety. The first issue of the *Journal* summarised the situation in this way:

> During the past two of three years, the new subject or, as some people might say, the newly christened subject, of Industrial Archaeology has aroused a degree of interest which has surprised even its own partisans.
>
> The study of the physical remains of an enormously rich and varied industrial past has proved an attraction to engineers, historians, economists, photographers, railway devotees, geographers, antique-dealers, schoolboys, professors, industrialists – a most encouraging and useful mixture of experts and amateurs, all anxious to take part in the urgent process of locating, recording, and, where possible, preserving the buildings and equipment which keep the story of technological development alive, properly documented and meaningful.[3]
>
> We see Industrial Archaeology, as a living, humane subject which provides a multitude of thought-provoking links between past and present. We agree entirely with two industrial journalists, when they tell us that 'every firm has its roots in the past, every factory, every industrial town is somehow invisibly but potentially scarred by that revolution; its ghosts can take up residence in the most modern glass-and-aluminium welfare and works-council ridden plant'.[4]

There was a good deal of suspicion of industrial archaeology at this time, and indeed for many years afterwards, together with some outright hostility. One can distinguish two main reasons for this. Archaeology had been a synonym for excavation for so long that above-ground material was not worthy of serious attention, and in the second place, anything dating only from the nineteenth or twentieth century was not yet old enough to have any archaeological value. For those who felt this way, industrial archaeology was at best ridiculous and at worst blasphemous.

It was therefore of crucial importance that the Council for British Archaeology should have taken industrial archaeology seriously from the beginning. Its Research and Advisory Committees on Industrial Archaeology played a valuable part in shaping official policy and in developing a public awareness of the need to view industrial monuments in exactly the same way as churches, castles or any other kind of historic building. The National Survey of Industrial Monuments, begun by the Ministry of Public Buildings and Works in 1963, was transferred to the CBA in 1966 and provided an opportunity which had never previously existed to take stock of the vast number of industrial remains which had survived in Britain and to select the most important for preservation. The CBA made industrial archaeology respectable.

By the late 1960s, the people who were taking an active interest in industrial archaeology had begun to fall into certain clearly defined groups. Before we look closely at these groups, it is worth noting that although the name industrial archaeology was easily accepted, its aficionados have always shown considerable reluctance to describe themselves as industrial archaeologists, and one wonders why. Is it that 'industrial archaeologist' is simply too long and too clumsy to be used with comfort, or is it, paradoxically, that the people who find a great deal of pleasure in industrial archaeology cannot really think of themselves as archaeologists? The problem is well worth further consideration.

There is no doubt that, from the beginning, there was a strong feedback into industrial archaeology from the lively and widespread devotion to local history which has been so marked in Britain since 1945. It is an approach to history that owes a great deal to the personality and scholarship of Professor W. G. Hoskins, who, with one foot in All Souls and the other in adult education classes, began to say firmly, clearly and bluntly soon after the war that what had been wrong with so much of local history in the past was that it was written in libraries, without the kind of information and perspective that could be obtained only by going out to see for oneself. Fieldwork was to be regarded as both a necessity and a pleasure. In his books, broadcasts and lectures, Professor Hoskins, the great apostle of fieldwork, made it abundantly clear that to attempt to carry out research in local history solely from printed or manuscript sources was to make it certain that a large number of mistakes would be made, many of them serious, and that misleading gaps would exist in the record.

The result of Professor Hoskins's campaign was that by the mid-Sixties, when industrial archaeology was beginning to strike roots, fieldwork in local history had become respectable. What is and was more in dispute is whether industrial archaeology should be considered a branch of local history or a branch of archaeology. One may well ask, 'Does it matter?', since archaeology is only one of many tools available to the historian, bearing in mind that some of the best work in both fields has been done by people to whom any distinction between history and archaeology, or, more precisely, between local history and industrial archaeology, has been entirely unimportant.

One such person is Robin Atthill, whose *Old Mendip*, first published in 1964, is both a classic of local history and a classic of industrial archaeology, according to one's point of view. It is the kind of book that can be written only by someone who knows the landscape as well as the documents, who has walked over every inch of the ground and who over many years has come to understand the interrelationship of the people and the district in a way which is difficult for an outsider to achieve. Mr Atthill, living in the middle of his material, but possessing the scholarship and the objectivity which allows him to understand what is significant about the local scene, is as sensitive to the

48. *No degree, no diploma. Boy from Portsmouth Grammar School during the 1964 excavation of Henry Cort's furnace at Funtley, Hampshire, where the puddling process for iron-making was pioneered in the 1770s. The excavation was carried out entirely by amateurs.*

aesthetic and poetic aspects of his subject as to the historical and technical. A book such as *Old Mendip*, and it has regrettably few equals, moves easily and naturally between local history and industrial archaeology. A passage from the chapter which tells the story of the nineteenth-century ironmasters, the Fussells of Mells, illustrates the style and the method. The Fussells' ironworks, very important in their day, were close to the family mansion, Nunney Court.

> The oldest parts of Nunney Court date from the time of Queen Anne, and some of the interior features, such as the recessed cupboards and the door handles, are from the same period, but the house as a whole did not benefit from the additions by the Fussells in the 1830s, nor by further additions in the 1930s. It is situated high above the little river, which here flows through a narrow combe, and to which a terraced garden and walks lead down. A few hundred yards upstream are the romantic ruins of the Castle, which actually belong to the Lord of the Manor, and below the Court the stream was dammed to provide power for the ironworks. There is an almost undecipherable jumble of ruined buildings lying along the river; at what was once the manager's house or office, one can still see the pay-hatch taking the place of one of the windows, and everywhere in the gardens the walls are topped with the remains of Fussells' worn-out grindstones, cut across like Dutch cheese or petrified half-moons.[5]

Old Mendip has been a successful book, reprinted several times. The reasons for its popularity are not hard to find, a fruitful combination of local pride, accurate fieldwork, good writing, and nostalgia, a fondness for passing glories. For this first category of industrial archaeologists, the group represented by Robin Atthill, the prime interest of the subject is its local history aspect. For them, industrial archaeology is a satisfying solid ingredient of local history, a fresh field to explore, something not overworked or with the life professionalised out of it.

A second group of industrial archaeology supporters probably has to be distinguished from the first, although the two overlap in many ways. These are the people whose primary interest is in social history. The social historians, like the local historians, include both professionals and amateurs, and their numbers have greatly increased during the past forty years. This particular wave of interest was already rising when Trevelyan published his *English Social History* in 1944, and it has shown no sign of declining in more recent years.

The social historians have found much to interest them in industrial archaeology. It is not difficult to think of examples of the cross-fertilisation of these two approaches to history. If, for instance, one reads the reports of the nineteenth-century Factory Inspectors, one can discover much that is of great value in allowing one to get the feel of industry at that time, information which helps one to put flesh on the archaeological bones. To regard industrial remains as dead objects, mere buildings and machinery, is to miss most of the point of industrial archaeology. The objects are there to stimulate one's historical awareness, and the more one knows about social conditions at the time, the greater and more rewarding that stimulus is likely to be.

In the textile mills of the eighteenth and early nineteenth centuries, for example, there were large numbers of children who were bullied, tired, frightened and, in some cases, no doubt, ill. One of the inevitable results of this, surely, is that they would continually have been wanting to relieve themselves. This thought causes one, both as an industrial archaeologist and as a social historian, to want to know something about the sanitary provisions in textile mills of the period. Yet, in reading even authoritative works on industrial conditions or industrial architecture during the nineteenth century, how often does one find the slightest mention or suggestion of this? In a rural environment, these unavoidable human problems, but given hundreds of people, adults as well as children, on a congested urban site, imprisoned in a factory for many hours on end, how and where were these important needs catered for?

If one has this kind of human consideration always in mind, then one will be automatically looking for relevant clues when one is visiting or studying a factory, just as one will be thinking about ventilation, temperature, lighting and noise. But in the conventional histories of industry in Victorian times one finds practically no mention of such things, as a glance at the index will soon show. The same absence of imagination and human feeling character- ises most of the guide books to medieval castles and manor houses, where only the abnormally curious will realise that the intriguing little stone bulges in the walls, high up above the moat, were put there for a purpose and not just as architectural ornament.

There can, however, be a problem in the case of people who are temperamentally and by training social historians, but who have developed a taste for industrial archaeology. They may feel – and a number of books and articles published during the past fifteen years illustrates this – that, because industrial archaeology has become fashionable, they are under some kind of obligation to include archaeological observations in what they write, but fail to integrate the two types of evidence, so that the archaeology tends to take the form of a half-hearted appendix. The problem is essentially one of proportion and emphasis. The archaeologist will start with what he finds and sees and work outwards from it; the social historian on the other hand is likely, unless he disciplines himself carefully, to begin with the documentary evidence and use the archaeological material as illustrations or light relief, not to be taken too seriously.

The third main group of industrial archaeologists might be defined as the people whose concern is mainly architectural. Architects who show an interest in industrial archaeology – and a number have been responsible for extremely valuable work in this field – usually do so for one of two reasons. One, more commonly found on the Continent than in Britain, is aesthetic. They find old industrial buildings, or some of them, beautiful to look at. If one takes a book like J. M. Richards and Eric de Maré's *The Functional Tradition* and asks oneself, 'What is it about these particular buildings that attracted the attention of these two experienced, imaginative observers?', one is faced with a complex problem. One of the main sources of appeal – whether it happens to be the main source it is difficult to say – is the sheer architectural charm of the buildings described and illustrated – simple, straightforward buildings, with no unnecessary frills, well suited to their purpose and often constructed of local materials.

Beauty is not a crime and the aesthetic appeal of old industrial buildings has been ignored for far too long in Britain, mainly, one suspects, because industry was associated with unpleasant things, smoke, soot, squalor, unemployment and poverty among them. It is certainly not a coincidence that industrial archaeology was born at a time of full employment and prosperity and when the modern, clean industries based on electricity and oil had begun to change the industrial image. But archaeology is not only or mainly a matter of aesthetics. Buildings which are far from beautiful in the conventional sense may be of great historical significance, and the elegant and the grand are often of no importance whatever.

The second reason why some architects have shown such a strong interest in industrial archaeology is that they are interested, as any good architect must be, in the function of buildings, in what they are or have been used for. No architect of any real quality can think of a building in isolation or as an abstraction. He necessarily and instinctively thinks of the building in its human and social context and because of this he feels drawn towards industrial archaeologists, who appear to him, rightly or wrongly, to be considering artifacts in the same way.

There is, of course, no such person as a typical architect or a typical industrial archaeologist but, if one had to choose an architect-archaeologist to serve as an example to his colleagues, it might well be Robert Clough, whose great book, *The Lead Smelting Mills of the Yorkshire Dales*, was published in 1962, when the industrial archaeology movement was still very much in its infancy. A Yorkshire architect in active practice, Mr Clough brought out this carefully researched and beautifully produced book on a subscription basis. One wonders whether such a procedure would still be possible and, for this reason, one should be grateful that the book appeared when it did, at something close to the eleventh hour.

The author admits, with refreshing honesty, that the real point and value of the book emerged only slowly as he went along. He tells us:

> As the survey was gradually completed it became clear that a most unusual and interesting group of buildings was being recorded for the first time; buildings of honest form and simple character, basically unaffected by any past style. However, I feel that the book is very much more than a record of stones and mortar; it is a record of a way of life illustrated by certain buildings which were necessary to make that way of life possible. I have endeavoured to look into the lives of these people, at all times somewhat aloof: people who lived, worked and died unnoticed in their remote surroundings. It is only by this understanding that one can fully appreciate the purpose of their buildings.[6]

Robert Clough was eager to express his indebtedness to J. M. Richards and Eric de Maré, whose influential book, *The Functional Tradition*, had been published four years earlier. He agreed completely with Richards' statement: 'Functionalism is not a creed peculiar to our own time, but the dominating ingredient of a deeply rooted tradition to which the anonymous architecture of every age bears witness'. His own task, as he saw it, was to survey and record the ruins of buildings, many of which had been disused for a century or more, and in this way to document an industry of which no first-hand memory remained. In words, drawings and photographs he aimed to preserve every available piece of information about the old lead smelting mills, so that the full story of this ancient industry could be told for the first time.

Architects, by definition, are people with a good visual sense who can draw and their humane, essentially practical interest in industrial archaeology has been responsible for much of the best work which has been done in industrial archaeology during the past twenty years, sometimes as pure individualism, sometimes as part of the collective effort of an organisation. One thinks, for instance, of what David Lloyd has done in connection with nineteenth-century railway stations within the framework of the Victorian Society, and of Kenneth Major's splendid surveys of waterwheels for the Society for the Protection of Ancient Monuments.

Our fourth group of people interested in industrial archaeology has been composed of what we might call enlightened industrial and commercial firms, many of whom, of course, are the owners of the material which industrial archaeologists are anxious to study and preserve. Such firms may decide to take or show an interest in history for a number of reasons. They may feel that it improves their image, by suggesting that they do not exist simply to make money, but that they are at bottom public spirited, even benevolent institutions. They may believe that a well-publicised respect for history and tradition helps to sell the product. The brewers have been outstanding in encouraging this approach. By creating an oak-beamed,

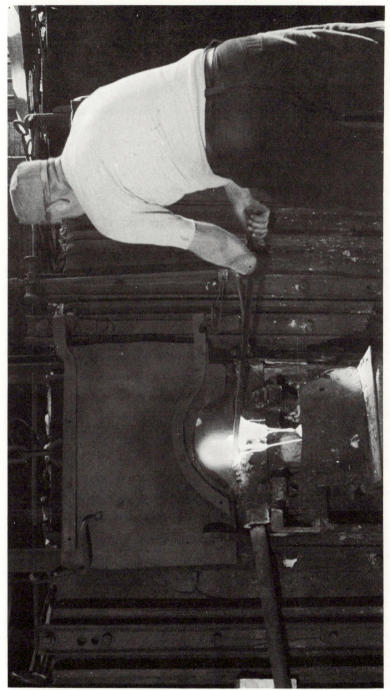

49. *The last iron-puddling furnace in the world at Thomas Walmsley and Sons Ltd, Bolton, photographed in action in 1972. The factory production of wrought-iron by this method has now come to an end and the furnace and associated equipment have been transferred to the Ironbridge Gorge Museum, where it is hoped to restart the old tradition of ironmaking. The furnace-man seen in this photograph is an important part of the archaeology.*

tankard, hunting-print atmosphere in their pubs, they have encouraged us to believe that we were the heirs to the swashbuckling, roistering habits of our deep-drinking ancestors, and this has probably been good for trade. And the more a brewery can point to its age, the more its customers may be inclined to forget what poor, weak beer it makes nowadays.

But, apart from these consciously commercial and sometimes cynical attachments to history, one does find among industrial people occasionally a perfectly genuine and disinterested attention to the past, either of their own firm or of the industry as a whole. Sometimes this happens because there is fortunately an eccentric running the firm or on its board, sometimes because history is felt to be good for company morale. In the 1960s the South Wales Electricity Board established a charming little museum at its apprentice school in Cardiff. It included an interesting collection of old electrical equipment which had been gathered together from the Board's area, backed up by a variety of documents and photographs. By putting this museum in the apprentice school and by bringing the story up to the present time, it was found possible to ensure that the apprentices became aware of the early days of their own industry and in this way to develop a dynamic attitude towards the past. One was saying, in effect, to the boys: 'This is the point at which you came in, but all this happened long before you were thought of, and changes will still be happening after you've retired.' More recently, the East Midlands Gas Board has created a similar, but more professional, museum at Leicester, to which the public is admitted.

What one finds at Cardiff and Leicester are essentially museum collections, with everything transferred to the museum from elsewhere. This is not industrial archaeology, which is concerned with items which have managed to survive on their original sites, but it is evidence of a respect for history on the part of the Boards concerned. Even so, the museum at Leicester is housed in what was formerly the office building of Leicester Gas Works, so that in this case one has a museum within a piece of industrial archaeology, a not uncommon occurrence nowadays. Near St Austell, for example, the English China Clays group has established an excellent museum of the industry within the area and buildings of a former clay works, in such a way that the relics of the clayworks form part of the museum. And, in 1959, Allied Ironfounders had shown a degree of enterprise which was quite exceptional at that time, by excavating and making accessible to the public Abraham Darby's 1777 iron furnace at Coalbrookdale, adjoining its own works.

One or two large, rich firms, such as Pilkingtons, at St Helens, and Guinness, in Dublin, have gone to considerable trouble and expense to set up a museum on a considerable scale. The Pilkington Glass Museum is, indeed, the second largest in the world devoted to this particular subject.

British industry, in fact, has a very good record in the matter of company museums. No other European country has as many, which may come as

50. *Chart Gunpowder Works, Faversham, during clearance operations in 1967. The excavation and recording at this important site was planned and carried out by members of the Faversham Society.*

something of a surprise to those whose experience leads them to believe that we are a land of philistines who live only for money and the present. A count made in 1964 and published in the first issue of the *Journal of Industrial Archaeology* showed a total of 69 company museums, with collections ranging from biscuit-making machinery to paints and varnishes, and from period corsetry to handmade nails.

These museums are fairly easy to discover. What is much more difficult, however, is to locate museum-pieces of machinery and equipment which are still preserved and in many cases still functioning on the premises where they were first installed, often a very long time ago. It is in these cases that the industrial archaeologist living in the area comes into his own, since he is in the position to develop his own intelligence system and, with luck, to find and possibly save an important item before it is destroyed. In fairness to industrial managements, it ought to be said that where destruction does take place, this is more likely to be as a result of ignorance or frustration than of deliberate vandalism. It is one of the unfortunate consequences of being in a country with such a long history of industrialisation and such a prodigious quantity of old equipment that it is important to find a good home for even the finest examples once the hour of superannuation and replacement has arrived.

Another regiment in the army of industrial archaeologists is composed of people whose main concern is with the history of technology as such, people who join the Newcomen Society. One can never be sure about anybody else's interests and motives, but it would be useful to circulate a questionnaire among members of the Newcomen Society in order to discover what the roots of their interest in the Society are, but, judging from its *Transactions* and *Bulletin* and from conversations with members, it would seem that a high proportion of them have a love of machinery as such, an engineer's love. There are undoubtedly many people of this type, mostly men, both inside and outside the Newcomen Society, and industrial archaeology has been able to attract quite a number of them. Usually, but not always, they are essentially practical people, not greatly interested in social or economic history, but prepared to take small doses of it from time to time.

One could continue identifying sub-groups of industrial archaeologists and those well-disposed towards industrial archaeology almost indefinitely. There are, for example, certain categories of civil servants, mainly employed by the Department of the Environment. There are people employed in museums, particularly in those connected with industry and technology. There are geographers of various kinds, for whom industrial archaeology yields important evidence of what man has done to shape the environment to meet his practical needs. There are historians whose concern is with social or economic histoyr, who realise the usefulness of testing their historical models against the physical evidence of the past. And there are, of course, tourists, who find industrial monuments a pleasant change from what the guide books have offered them in the past.

There is an important difference between industrial archaeologists and most of the other kinds of archaeologists with which this book has been concerned. Very little excavation-archaeology has ever been carried out by one person working on his own, mainly because shifting earth, sand and rubbish is a laborious business and, unless the circumstances are unusually favourable, one cannot accomplish a great deal single-handed. Just occasionally, an individual with an exceptional amount of energy will achieve the impossible, as James Stevens Cox did at Ilchester. But the conditions of this one-man dig at part of the Roman town are not often likely to be repeated, since Mr Cox's site was literally in his back garden and he was able to slip away to do a little archaeology from time to time, much as other people look after their flowers and vegetables. He was, in any case, a man of the Napoleon type who required very little in the way of rest or sleep.

Archaeologists whose material is above ground are in quite a different situation from the excavators and most of them experience few problems in working as individuals. Most of them, in fact, seem to prefer it this way. One of the greatest pleasures of exploring and studying old churches, for instance, is the peace of doing something entirely alone. It may be that part of the paranoic hatred shown by the excavators towards the men with metal-detectors is that the metal-detector men are loners, people who stubbornly refuse to be organised. And, as most of us know from our schooldays, anyone who scorns team games is an anti-social heretic of the worst kind, to be attacked and suppressed in every possible way.

Industrial archaeology, unlike dirt archaeology, has never found any serious difficulty in accommodating its individualists. They were there in the early 1960s and they are still there, pleasing themselves and contriving to do a great deal of useful work in the process. One remembers with gratitude and admiration the pioneering efforts of Brian Lamb, a Manchester school-master, who devoted his spare time to studying the Peak Forest Canal and Tramway; Richard Storey, who concentrated on old breweries and cinemas in Hertfordshire; Donald Cross, who moved on from the Lymington salt industry to a wide range of other rural industries in Hampshire; Dorothy Vinter, who spent many years tracking down and recording the archaeology of the Bristol Coalfield. And there were many others of the same type, following their enthusiasms wherever they happened to lead and educating themselves continuously in the process.

The chief value of the *Journal of Industrial Archaeology* was that it provided this very miscellaneous collection of people with an opportunity to publish the results of their work, which would otherwise in all probability have remained completely unknown. There was no other journal which catered for their particular needs. It is interesting now to look back on the subjects

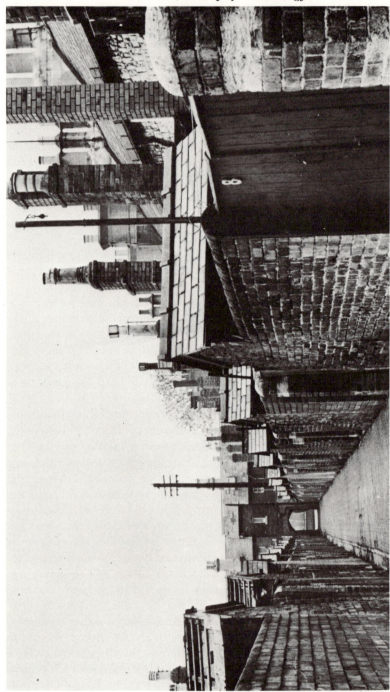

51. *The industrial archaeologist's raw material. The Railway Village, Swindon, as it was in the mid-1960s. Built in the 1840s and 1850s to provide accommodation for men employed at the Great Western Works, these houses were of much higher quality than those being put up by speculative builders at the same period.*

which found their way into print through the *Journal* during its first year, 1964–65.

The titles of the articles published in the first issue, May 1964, were: 'An Open-Air Museum for the North-East'; 'Early Fulling Stocks in Gloucester-shire'; 'A Survival of the Wiltshire Paper Industry'; 'Company Museums'; 'Surviving Evidence of the New Forest Charcoal Burning Industry'; 'The Archaeology of the Bristol Coalfield'; 'Industrial Archaeology Abroad: Belgium'; and 'Early Landing Places in the Port of Southampton'.

No. 2, August 1964, was a rather larger issue. It began with 'The Newcomen Society and Industrial Archaeology', and continued with 'The Blorenge'; 'The Photographic Aspects of Industrial Archaeology'; 'Memoirs of a Branch Line Archaeologist'; 'The New Department of Technology, Bristol City Museum'; 'Birmingham's Gun Quarter and its Workshops'; 'The National Trust and the Stratford-upon-Avon Canal'; 'The Clapham Engine'; 'The Industries of Witney'; 'Survivals of 17th and 18th century Blast-Furnaces'; and 'The History of Textiles'.

By the time No. 3 appeared, in November 1964, the Editor was able to write, 'The *Journal* is now in the fortunate position of being almost embarrassed by the number of contributions which are coming forward. We shall do our best to publish them with a minimum of delay, giving preference to those which deal with areas of Britain which have so far been inadequately, if at all, represented in our pages. The most notable gaps at present appear to be the North-East, East Anglia, and the South-East, and any material relating to these parts of the country will be especially welcome.'[7]

In this issue there appeared 'Some Cornish Industrial Artifacts in the United States of America'; 'Industrial Archaeology in the North-West, 1960–1964'; 'The History of New Lanark'; 'Survivals of the Brinore Tramroad in Brecknockshire'; 'A Proposal to Establish National Parks of Industrial Archaeology'; 'A Working Library for the Industrial Archaeology Abroad: Germany'.

The first year of publication was rounded off, in January 1965, with 'The Catcliffe Glassworks'; 'Three Eighteenth Century Scottish Ironworks'; 'The Festiniog Railway Archives and Museum'; 'Industrial Archaeology and Schools of Architecture'; and 'Hitch's Patent Bricks'.

Of the 30 articles listed above, only 9 were by people holding some kind of academic post. As time went on, the proportion steadily changed, until by 1974, ten years after the first issue appeared, it was comparatively rare to find a major contribution which came from anyone who was not employed in a university or other institution of higher education. The academics, one might say, had taken over, leaving the amateurs to find an outlet for their work where they could, sometimes, with luck, in the transactions of the county archaeological societies, sometimes in the journals and bulletins put out by local industrial archaeology societies. More will be said about these societies and their journals later, but for the moment we shall take a closer look at who these early industrial archaeologists were, using the clues afforded by the brief biographies in the *Journal*. Like the Victorian obituaries from which we quoted earlier, these personal details give a useful impression of the kind of person who has been active in industrial archaeology at different periods, and in some cases, alas, future historians may find the biographies more valuable than the articles to which they relate.

Here, at any rate, are the contributors to three issues of *Industrial Archaeology*, one in 1966 and the others in 1968 and 1974.

In 1966[8] the Editor was able to gather the following personal details about his contributors:

Miss S. R. Amner. Taught art for a number of years. Writes on gardening and lives near Nottingham. Was once the plant recorder for Holland, Lincs. Now the thunderstorm recorder for part of the Nottingham area. Hobbies include local history, needlework and winemaking.

D. E. Bick. Leeds graduate. Chief designer of specialised industrial hydraulic equipment. Has been studying Welsh metal mines for the past ten years. Interested in all types of old machinery and prime movers. Vintage motorist – 80,000 miles to date.

Crispin Gill. Assistant editor of *The Western Morning News*, Plymouth, and author of *Plymouth: A New History*, to be published in November. Lives on the outskirts of Yelverton, ten miles from the city.

E. P. Griffith. Chairman of Hexham Historical Group. Member of Hexham R.D.C. Member of the Society for the Protection of Ancient Buildings for 25 years. Now busy with a survey of watermills of Northumberland for the Society's general Index.

John R. Hume. Took degree in applied chemistry in Glasgow. Now assistant lecturer in Department of Economic History, University of Strathclyde, with special responsibility for the teaching of the history of science and technology. Chairman of the Scottish Railway Preservation Society.

(a) *W. Branch Johnson* and (b) his father-in-law, *W. E. Pickerill*. (a) Fifty years a journalist. Since 1945 has concentrated almost entirely on the history and topography of Hertfordshire, where he lives. Completing a survey of pre-1900 industrial monuments for the Herts. County Council. Has also written an historical study of 880 Hertfordshire pubs (b) Son of a journeyman hatter. b. Manchester 1882. Became gas-engine fitter. Joined Aeronautical Inspection Directorate, 1915. Retired 1845. Speciality was screw threads, but his wide variety of interests ranged from politics to horology. d. 1966.

J. Kenneth Major. Practising architect. Lives in Berkshire, works in London. Trained at King's College, Newcastle-upon-Tyne. Lethaby Scholar of the Society for the Protection of Ancient Buildings (1952). Takes a particular interest in windmills and watermills.

Walter M. Stephen. Edinburgh graduate. Teaches geography at Balwearie Secondary School, Kirkcaldy, Fife. Interests include archaeological excavation with groups of schoolchildren and social changes resulting from the opening of the Forth Bridge.

Arthur E. J. Went. Doctorate in zoology. Londoner. Scientific adviser to the Fisheries Division, Department of Agriculture and Fisheries, Dublin. Expert on the past and present of the Irish fishing industry.

One's first comment on the subjects of these ten portraits might well be, 'A good mixed bag', and after that one might feel inclined to note that only one of the contributors worked at a university and that the others fitted into no particular pattern at all. No profile of a typical industrial archaeologist emerges from the information we are given about these people. They are clearly individuals, doing what interests them and bringing to the subject a wide range of talent, training and experience.

We move on to 1968[9] to see how, if at all, the situation has changed over two years, as industrial archaeology becomes a more settled feature of the national life. This is what we find under the heading, 'Notes on Contributors'.

G. T. Bloomfield. Lecturer in Department of Geography, University of Auckland. Before going to New Zealand in 1964, was at University of Nottingham, where he wrote a thesis on the Location of the British Motor Vehicle, Cycle and Aircraft Industry. Has made several visits to Fiji. Soon to carry out research on the archaeology of the sugar industry. Hopes soon to publish an outline survey of important industrial monuments and relics in the Auckland area.

G. C. Cullingham. Borough Surveyor and Engineer, Royal Borough of New Windsor since 1965. Was formerly at Herne Bay, Canterbury and Bexhill. Has done a plan of urban history and a history of water supply. Main interest is sanitary engineering.

H. D. Gribbon, B.Com.Sc., Ph.D. Civil servant in Belfast. Has done research at Department of Economic and Social History, Queen's University, Belfast. At the moment is preparing a history of waterpower of Ulster and a history of the Irish Linen Board.

Arthur Percival. Born in North Kensington in 1933. Lived for a time in Sandwich before settling in Faversham, in 1959. Worked in the London

52. The Railway Village at Swindon during restoration and modernisation in the early 1970s. Industrial archaeologists had much detailed recording work to do before these Victorian houses were taken over by the local Council and made suitable for late 20th century tenants. A comparison between the old and the new provides an excellent illustration of the difference between 19th and 20th century living standards.

County Council Members' Library for six years before taking up his present appointment as Librarian of the Civic Trust. He has been the Hon. Secretary of the Faversham Society since its formation in 1962.

P. J. Povey. Post Office engineer since 1947. Started Taunton P.O. Museum in 1957. Has several ideas for improving it, but as yet no concrete plans are suitable for publication.

Dorothy Vinter. Oxford English degree. Taught in London, West Indies and Bristol. Reginald Taylor Prize, 1955, for paper on the naval prison at Stapleton, Bristol, during the Napoleonic Wars. Writes articles on local history for two Gloucestershire papers.

It is a well-known phenomenon in journalism that every paper and periodical eventually attracts the kind of contributor the editor wants, although it may take a little time for the style and aims of the publication to be understood. But that some degree of self-selection among contributors takes place there can be no doubt, and this has to be kept in mind when looking through the file of the *Journal of Industrial Archaeology*, which soon became *Industrial Archaeology* and a few years later *Industrial Archaeology Review*. Once it became widely known that the Editor was particularly anxious to publish the work of amateurs, which in this case, since industrial archaeology had no real professionals, had to be interpreted as 'people not holding academic posts in subjects relevant to industrial archaeology', articles written by amateurs were certain to flow in. With a new Editor, himself a distinguished economic historian, soon to occupy a Chair in the subject, the ratio of academic to non-academic contributors changed considerably. This is not the place to discuss whether this was a good or a bad thing to happen. The point is that it did happen and anyone who uses the List of Contributors section of *Industrial Archaeology* from 1969 onwards has to make a different kind of assumption and allowance. Up the 1969, he is likely to conclude, unless he understands the editorial situation, that non-academics were more important than perhaps they really were; after 1969, he may need to weight the evidence in a different way. All editors have their prejudices and preferences and it is good that this should be so.

But, with the new tradition established, here are the contributors for August 1974.[10]

W. E. Minchinton is Professor and Head of the Department of Economic History at the University of Exeter. As far as his interests in IA are concerned, he is Chairman of the Exeter IA Group, and among his range of publications are *Industrial Archaeology in Devon* (Devon County Council, 2nd ed. 1973) and *Devon at work: past and present* (David and Charles, 1974) and, with John Perkins, *Tidemills of Devon and Cornwall* (Exeter IA Group, 1971).

53. *The industrial archaeologist's raw material. Upper part of the façade of the former South-Western Hotel, Southampton, one of Britain's foremost hotels in the great days of the transatlantic liners and now downgraded as South-Western House to shipping and a regional BBC headquarters. Built in two parts, 1865 and 1902, its size and internal grandeur testifies to its one-time importance and prosperity. It has so far been most inadequately documented and recorded.*

S. J. Telford is research assistant in historical geography at North London Polytechnic and is at present into certain aspects of the development of the Northumberland coalfield up to 1850.

E. C. Ruddock is on the staff of the Department of Architecture at the University of Edinburgh.

Gavin Bowie is at present doing research towards a Ph.D. at the Institute of Irish Studies, Queen's University, Belfast, on the use of prime-movers, and especially stationary steam engines, in Irish industry in the eighteenth and nineteenth centuries. During the summer of 1972 he undertook industrial archaeology survey work for An Fores Forbatha, the National Institute for Physical Planning and Construction Research.

Tom Donnelly graduated in Economic History at the University of Strathclyde, continuing postgraduate studies at the University of Aberdeen. He is now a lecturer in Economic History at Lancaster Polytechnic.

It is dangerous to generalise, but what probably happened between 1969 and 1974 was that the amateurs in industrial archaeology concentrated their efforts and their interests increasingly on fieldwork and on various kinds of local enterprise, and the professionals, that is, the full-time academics, began to see themselves more and more as occupying the rôle of synthesisers and interpreters. Something very close to a two-layer system has been developing, not very different, perhaps, from what one has already seen in the case of excavation-archaeology. One might call the two layers the diggers and collectors and the processors.

What one cannot disregard, however, in any survey of the growth of industrial archaeology in Britain is its social or gregarious aspect, its club element. This does not necessarily have very much to do with scholarship. It reflects simply the wish of like-minded people to meet one another and to do things together. In that sense, an industrial archaeology society is no different from a bridge club or a gardening association. A common interest brings the members together and, so long as the organisation is run with reasonable efficiency and recruitment balances out the inevitable wastage, there is usually no great difficulty in arranging an acceptable programme year after year.

In 1971 the *Industrial Archaeologists' Guide* listed 67 societies or groups in the British Isles which were specifically concerned with industrial archaeology. They were not evenly distributed over the country and some were undoubtedly in a more flourishing state than others, but they could be taken as representing the popular interest in industrial archaeology at the local level. For the record, it has to be said that it is unlikely that more than a third of these societies are still really active. 1971 probably represents the highest point of what one might call the hobby interest in industrial archaeology. The societies listed in the *Guide* were of two kinds, those which were off-shoots of larger societies concerned with history or archaeology in a wider sense, and societies which had come into being solely to cater for the interests of people who were attracted by industrial archaeology.

As an example of the first group one could select the Industrial Archaeology Section of the Devonshire Association for the Advancement of Science, Literature and Art. 'The policy of this section,' says the *Guide*, 'is to promote the discovery, recording and understanding of industrial and technical remains in the county of Devon. Current studies include Dartmoor and the Tamar Valley mining and mineral processing; Dartmoor granite working; agricultural mechanisation; watermills; limekilns; roadside stones; china clay extraction; disused tramways.'

Typical of the second group was the Sussex Industrial Archaeology Study Group, 'founded at the end of 1967, to carry out research and recording and to collaborate in establishing an open-air museum for the Weald and Downland at West Dean, near Chichester. Projects include surveys at

Brighton and Hove; natural power; full power; toll-houses; railway architecture; breweries and malthouses; ice houses.'

A lively, well-run society had a good research programme, in which members could take an active part; organised excursions; lectures and conferences; and published a newsletter or bulletin two or three times a year and a more elaborate journal once a year. It is interesting to notice that the relatively few societies which in 1971 were doing all these things have survived and are still thriving, whereas those which were content with a less ambitious programme ten years ago have either faded away or are in a languishing state today. The really good societies in 1971 are still the really good societies – Bristol Industrial Archaeological Society (BIAS); the Greater London Industrial Archaeology Society (GLIAS); the Historical Metallurgy Group; the North-Western Society for Industrial Archaeology and History; Salisbury and South Wiltshire Industrial Archaelogy Society; Sussex Industrial Archaeology Society are the leaders today.

It is difficult to estimate how many people at any given time have been members of the industrial archaeology societies which have been formed for their benefit. Suppose, however, that each of the 67 societies which existed in 1971 had a minimum membership of fifty people – it would have been difficult for it to function effectively with fewer than this. In that case, the supporters of the subject who were organised in this way would have totalled rather more than 3,000 people, which is probably fairly close to the right figure. By no means all of these people will have been actively engaged in fieldwork. Some will have paid a subscription in order to support what they feel to be a good cause or to oblige their friends, others will have joined for the sake of the excursions, the lectures or the company. Let us say that at the peak of its appeal as a spare-time activity industrial archaeology was able to count on a maximum of 1,500 front-line troops, working on their own or as members of groups. It is something like this number of people, over a period of about fifteen years, who have carried out the astonishing amount of locating and recording which we are only now beginning to digest.

There are, of course, quite as many reasons for going in for industrial archaeology as for going in for gambling or golf, and no two people are motivated in precisely the same way. For some, no doubt, the attraction is the same as for some excavators – the satisfaction of a sporting instinct to follow clues which may lead to the discovery of forgotten or hidden objects. For others, there is the pleasure of getting one's historical bearings through tangible, real objects, rather than from books, or finding veterans who will reminisce about their working days. Others again see industrial archaeology as a splendid opportunity to indulge a taste for photography or drawing.

What one can say with fair certainty is that the great majority of industrial archaeologists carry out their chosen tasks within twenty miles of their home. Some of them may occasionally work further afield, usually as part of a course

54. *Rear view of South-Western House, Southampton, showing part of the now abandoned Terminus Station, which allowed transatlantic passengers to go straight from the train to the hotel. Aesthetically, the industrial archaeologist's material often leaves a good deal to be desired.*

organised by a university extra-mural department, but these are the exceptionally adventurous. For most people, this is a special kind of local history, researched, talked about and written up by local people. It is very unusual to find someone from, say, Birmingham, engaged on fieldwork in Glasgow or Great Yarmouth. The peripatetic archaeologist working at his hobby is much more common in the excavation than in the industrial kind of archaeology. One important and rarely commented on reason for this is that industrial archaeology has so few people who can be described as students. Only two British universities have undergraduate degree courses which include a substantial component of industrial archaeology. A truly student work-force does not exist, in the way it does for Roman or prehistoric archaeology.

Not that the absence of the conventional kind of student, with a degree and a career in mind, matters very much. Some of the people who devote their energies to studying the remains of yesterday's methods of making things and of moving goods and people from one place to another may do so for mainly scholarly purposes, that is, in the hope of being able to improve our knowledge of the industrial past, but far more are likely to do so for the sake of their own personal education, to reach a better understanding of how our ancestors earned their living and how they adapted themselves to changing technology and conditions of work.

If there has been any falling off of interest in recent years, the main cause could be a feeling that all the discoveries have been made, that the excitement of coming across something new is going to happen less and less often, and that the only thing that remains for the future is to visit Ironbridge, Crofton pumping station and other holy places. During the past twenty years or so, what still remains of eighteenth and nineteenth century industrial and transport relics and sites has been pretty thoroughly pin-pointed. There must now be very few buildings or pieces of machinery dating from the First Industrial Revolution which have been overlooked. The Age of Steam, one can now say, has been well recorded and, when one thinks of the situation in 1950, this represents a notable triumph. The industrial archaeologists can reasonably claim to have broadened both historical awareness and the definition of history.

What has not yet happened on anything like the same scale or with the same publicity or esteem is the extension of industrial archaeology into the twentieth century. What was new and stimulating in the Sixties has become fossilised in the Seventies. The early days of the new industries – electricity, aviation, aluminium, automobiles, oil, petrochemicals, synthetic fibres, computers, telecommunications – have so far received only a fraction of the devoted attention which has been bestowed on the archaeology of coal, canals, railways and steam. It cannot be accidental that the local societies – GLIAS and BIAS are good examples – which have deliberately and energetically widened their scope and entered the field of twentieth century industries should have been the ones which are doing even better now than they were ten years ago.

The principal attempt to enlist the help of the local societies in a national project failed to produce the response that was hoped of it. The project was and still is the National Record of Industrial Monuments, which grew out of the CBA's initiative in setting up a nationwide survey of these monuments in the early 1960s.[11] At that time there were no local industrial societies and the CBA had to rely on its own Regional Groups to circulate the special cards that had been printed. There was, however, no proper organisation to receive and file the completed cards and therefore no way of referring to them. Some of the bundles found their way to the Ministry of Works and some to the CBA and it was impossible to consult them, because nobody knew what was where.

Eventually, the whole enterprise was handed over to the Centre for the Study of the History of Technology at the University of Bath, which proceeded to xerox in triplicate and classify each card as it came in. One copy went to the CBA, one to the National Buildings Record and the third stayed behind in Bath as the file copy of the National Record of Industrial

Monuments. Once some degree of system had been introduced into the enterprise, certain defects were soon apparent. Two stood out particularly clearly – the cards varied enormously in quality and the distribution of the sites to which they referred was extremely uneven over the country as a whole. The cards, lamented Dr Buchanan, who was in charge of the Bath Centre, 'range from those which are so badly written as to be unintelligible or so vague as to be useless, at one end of the scale, to the carefully written, drawn and illustrated cards at the other end, packing in a great deal of useful information'.[12]

The unevenness of the record, the other major failing, is illustrated by a county-by-county league table, published in *Industrial Archaeology* in 1966.[13] Shropshire, with 303 completed cards, had a runaway lead, followed by Glamorgan with 175, and Yorkshire and Somerset with 120 apiece. Gloucestershire, Hertfordshire, Essex, Northamptonshire, Huntingdonshire, Herefordshire, Westmorland, Cardigan and Radnor all registered zero. There were no figures for Northern Ireland or the Isle of Man, where independent surveys were in progress. The poor showing of Hertfordshire was accounted for by the fact that the cards for this county, 300 of them, had been temporarily lost by the Ministry of Works.

A year later, however, the position had not changed a great deal.[14] Shropshire had stuck at 303, but Somerset was now 265 and Yorkshire 241. A gigantic cache of Hertfordshire cards had appeared from somewhere, 613, instead of 300 as previously, and Nottinghamshire and Lincolnshire had both done rather well, with 210 and 114 respectively. There was still only one card from Cambridgeshire and Sussex, but Cardigan, with 1, Huntingdon and Herefordshire with 2 and Gloucestershire with 4 had managed to emerge from total obscurity.

Another grave fault with the scheme, as Dr Buchanan pointed out, was that 'the time lag between recording a site in the field and placing an appropriate card in the Record is frequently so great that the information can never be relied upon to be contemporary'.[15] All in all, the locals were not behaving as they should. Yet – and this was the snag – there appeared to be no way of managing without them. For this reason, they had to be wooed, teased and inspired, rather than castigated. Only if they agreed to co-operate in a properly disciplined way – and apart from esprit de corps and patriotism, there was no particular reason why they should – could the National Register be made something worth having. The appeal to their good sense and co-operative spirit was made in these terms:

The value of the NRIM in the last resort will be in its comprehensiveness. As it approaches completion it will be a unique source of information for industrial remains in this country and will be available for the compilation of local histories, industrial distribution maps and so on. Otherwise forgotten industrial processes and landmarks will be filed for posterity and, as to the historian all information is good information, the Record will be a valuable archive. This is a longer-term objective than the short-term aim of selecting industrial monuments for preservation, but it is not less valuable. To fulfil it, however, the NRIM will continue to rely utterly on the enthusiasm and the co-operation of individuals and societies who are convinced of its value. It is much to be hoped that people who are at present sitting on piles of completed record cards in the hope of incubating books and other publications will let us borrow the cards for the extension of our Record. For, while we would not deny that there is a great deal more to industrial archaeology than the completion of record cards, the construction of a really comprehensive and integrated National Record should retain a high priority in the endeavours of serious industrial archaeologists.[16]

This might be described, perhaps, as an inspirational reprimand, the general addressing his troops at a time when the battle is not going too well and when a big final effort is required to achieve victory. The military metaphor is apt only up to a point, however, since in industrial archaeology the commanders have no sanctions or punishments with which to make sure that their orders are obeyed. Much as they might like to, they cannot in fact command. They can only persuade and encourage and, given the amount of work that exists to be done, this may well be a frustrating experience. In the passage just quoted there are two phrases which expose the reality of the situation. One is the reference to people 'sitting on piles of completed record cards', and the other is the concept of 'serious industrial archaeologists'.

When considering any kind of partnership, one always has to ask how equal it is. Are the interests of both parties equally balanced or does A need B more than B needs A? In the present case, and possibly for British archaeology as a whole, it may well be that the professionals, as represented by the Centre for the Study of the History of Technology, needed the amateurs more than the amateurs needed them and that the amateurs, the freelance enthusiasts and the members of local groups, were rather enjoying the situation. To what extent they could be placed in the category of 'serious industrial archaeologists' is another matter. What, after all, is a 'serious industrial archaeologist'? Is he someone who has set himself the major lifelong task of bringing his knowledge and techniques up to professional standards? Or someone fighting for a cause? Or simply a serious-minded person who happens to have been attracted to industrial archaeology? Or someone who respects the status and authority of the professionals and behaves as they expect him to behave?

Industrial archaeology, as we have seen it develop in Britain, has been a wonderful laboratory in which to explore and examine the amateur-

55. Site of 19th century lead-smelting works at Charterhouse-on-Mendip, Somerset. A group of schoolchildren helping to survey the flue leading from the base of the chimney.

professional relationship. One can observe the longings of the academics for something they are given to calling 'organised industrial archaeology', in which ground is mapped out, hierarchies established and acknowledged, tasks allocated, conferences arranged, periodicals edited, promotions ob-tained and books and articles written, exactly in the way it all happens in real academic subjects like economics and physics. One can be fascinated and sometimes amused by the frenzied efforts of university people to prove to themselves and to those who control educational spending that industrial archaeology is, or could be transformed into a true 'discipline', a worthy field of higher study.

'Ultimately,' Philip Riden has written, 'the subject must stand as a branch of archaeology, not history.'[17] 'Before 19th century archaeology,' he goes on, curiously excluding 20th century archaeology from consideration, 'can become more than marginally valuable to the historian and more than a joke to all but a few archaeologists, there must be changes in the present state of the subject. The hundreds of dedicated amateurs throughout the country, with enormous reserves of energy and enthusiasm, but limited skill and resources, should be persuaded to join their country archaeological societies and work within the framework of archaeology as a whole.'[18]

No doubt, but who is to do the persuading? Whether one joins this or that society or no society at all is a matter of tradition and incentive. Words like 'must' and phrases like 'should be persuaded' are not practical politics and reflect a strange view of human nature. It is quite possible that, for many people, industrial archaeology was a passing intellectual fashion and that, as a fashion, it is already past its peak. But it is equally possible that those who join a lively, well-organised society, such as GLIAS or BIAS, actually prefer it to their county archaeological society and that the alternative to GLIAS or BIAS, so far as they are concerned, is nothing at all. One cannot shuffle people about from one society to another like pawns on a chessboard. Everything Philip Riden says may be entirely logical and in its way sensible. The only thing wrong with such an approach is that it has no chance of working.

Everything, one might say, looks different from the other end of the telescope, and Mr Riden and Dr Buchanan are looking at industrial archaeo-logy from the academic end, where values, priorities and ambitions tend to be a little different from those one finds during a happy weekend surveying a hop warehouse near London Bridge with one's friends, where the wish to do a good job and the enjoyment of the company are likely to be very evenly balanced.

Elsewhere,[19] I have suggested that industrial archaeology in Britain has already passed through two stages of development and may now be well into a third. Stage One, I felt, had ended in about 1960. It had been the period of the true pioneers and crusaders, a very small and curiously assorted body whose main function, as they saw it, was to create a public conscience about the rapid disappearance of nineteenth century industrial buildings and equipment. They usually indulged in a fair amount of necessary exaggeration and, on occasion, more than a little sentimentality, a way that all trail-blazers must, but they performed an invaluable publicity service for 'industrial archaeology', an impossible phrase with great shock-value.

Stage Two, as I saw it, was an affair of the Sixties and the very early Seventies. It was distinguished by the creation of a network of amateur groups engaging in industrial archaeology as a hobby, by the beginnings of a rudimentary Register of Industrial Monuments, by a spate of books on the subject, by a Journal, and, not the least significant, by the belated growth of academic interest in the subject, starting in university extra-mural departments and penetrating in a tentative and rather apprehensive manner into departments of history and economics. Stage Three, in which we now uncomfortably find ourselves, occurs when it becomes obvious that stocktaking has to take place. The mass of material collected during Stages One and Two is weighed and subjected to critical examination to see what it really adds up to, what new contribution it makes to knowledge. This is the point at which one is forced to admit that the honeymoon is over, and that one is destined to have an inevitable, but one hopes creative period of heartsearching and quarrels, of which we have given some evidence above.

It is interesting to observe that industrial archaeologists find themselves now in very much the same situation as any other kinds of archaeologists – confronted with a forbidding mass of notes, drawings and photographs in urgent need of digestion and interpretation. This, however, is essentially a professional job, and to what extent amateurs are likely to be able to or willing to take a hand in it remains to be seen. From this point of view, the amateur-professional partnership which has been the great British achievement, for all the creaking and rattling that has been heard from time to time, may already be becoming less of a reality.

The amateur's strongest card has always been, however, that he costs nothing, and that, in these harsh days when archaeology has to take its share of severe cuts in public spending, is not to be ignored or underplayed. Archaeology, in order to continue to thrive and develop in Britain, may have to think of much more effective ways of using unpaid enthusiasm and expertise for tasks which have hitherto been considered a professional monopoly. In archaeology, as in everything else, necessity is a wonderful mother of invention.

Notes

INTRODUCTION

1. *A Hundred and Fifty Years of Archaeology*, p. 104.
2. *Allen v Thorn Electrical Industries, Ltd.* 1907.
3. *My First Hundred Years*, 1963, p. 189.
4. Ibid, p. 190.
5. *Spadework*, 1953, p. 12.
6. *Archaeology in the Field*, 1953, p. 8.
7. Presidential Address to the Society of Antiquaries, *Antiquaries Journal*, 1975, vol. LV, part I, p. 7.
8. *Antiquaries Journal*, 'Excavations at Winchester, 1969. Eighth Interim Report', p. 227.
9. Ibid, pp. 277–8.
10. Ibid, p.278.
11. *Antiquaries Journal*, vol. LV, part I, 1975, p. 5.
12. Ibid, p. 6.
13. On the characteristics of the professions, near-professions and would-be professions, see Kenneth Hudson, *The Jargon of the Professions*, 1978, pp. 7–12.
14. Myres, op. cit., p. 6.
15. Myres, op. cit., pp. 7–8.
16. Ibid, p. 7.

CHAPTER 1

1. *Somersetshire Archaeological and Natural History Society: Proceedings during the Years 1849–50*, vol. 1, 1851.
2. On this, see Stuart Piggott, 'County Archaeological Societies', *Antiquity*, June 1968.
3. *Somersetshire Archaeological and Natural History Society. Proceedings during the Years 1948–9*, vol. XCIV, 1950, p. 28.
4. Year of the Society's foundation.
5. Vol. X, 1930, p. 393.
6. Vol. I, 1921, p. 76.
7. Vol. II, 1922, p. 391.
8. Vol. II, 1922, pp. 390–1.
9. Vol. II, 1922, p. 68.

10. Vol. II, 1922, p. 69.
11. Vol. XIII, 1933, p. 173.
12. Vol. II, 1922, p. 269.
13. The well-known journal on early archaeology, *Matériaux pour l'histoire de l'homme.*
14. Vol. VII, 1927, pp. 185–6.
15. Vol. XXI, 1941, p. 84.
16. Vol. I, 1921, p. 242.
17. Vol. XII, 1933, pp. 474–5.
18. Vol. IX, 1929, p. 46.
19. Vol. VI, 1926, p. 451.
20. Vol. IX, 1929, p. 251.
21. Vol. XVII, 1937, p. 449.
22. Vol. XIV, 1934, p. 196.
23. Vol. XIII, 1933, p. 64.
24. Vol. I, 1921, p. 145.
25. Vol. IV, 1924, p. 279.
26. Vol. IV, 1924, p. 162.
27. Vol. VIII, 1928, p. 107.
28. Vol. XXI, 1941, p. 241.

CHAPTER 2

1. *Proceedings of the Society of Antiquaries of London*, vol. X, 1859, p. 144.
2. Now gone.
3. *The Antiquarian*, vol. I, 1871, p. 79.
4. *The Antiquarian*, vol. I, 1871, p. 21.
5. Ibid, p. 95.
6. In 1841 *The Times* had a circulation of 28,000 and in 1854 55,000. Its nearest rival, the *Morning Post*, had 6,600. In that year the *Daily Telegraph* was started and a few years later it became the first newspaper to sell for a penny. The halfpenny *Daily Mail* began publication in 1896 and by 1900 this was selling a million copies a day.
7. Joan Evans, *Time and Chance: the story of Arthur Evans and his forebears*, 1943, p. 108.
8. Ibid, p. 158.
9. *The Life-Work of Lord Avebury (Sir John Lubbock), 1834–1913*, ed. Adrian Grant (his daughter), 1924, p. 14.
10. Ibid, pp. 23–4.
11. Ibid, p. 21.
12. 6 May 1871, p. 6.
13. Ibid, 20 May 1871, p. 13.
14. The best general survey of the part played by the State in this field up to the mid-1930s is Graham Clark's 'Archaeology and the State', *Antiquity*, vol. 8, no. 32, December 1934.
15. The best account of the work carried out at Silchester from the 1860s onwards is to be found in George S. Boon, *Silchester: the Roman Callium*, 1974.

16. They are preserved at Reading Museum.

17. Silchester is about eight miles south-west of Reading.

18. Gray was born in 1872 at Lichfield, 'where his father was connected with the cathedral' (*Proceedings* of the Somersetshire Archaeological and Natural History Society, vol. 107, 1963, p. 11). After leaving Cranborne Chase, he spent a short time with the Pitt-Rivers Museum in Oxford and then, in 1901, went to Taunton, where he was Secretary and Keeper until 1949.

19. *Excavations in Cranborne Chase*, vol. 3, 1901, p. 9.

20. Quoted in Joan Evans, *Time and Chance*, 1943, p. 270.

CHAPTER 3

1. *A Hundred and Fifty Years of Archaeology*, 1975, p. 22.

2. Ibid, p. 22.

3. *Autobiography and Letters*, vol. II, p. 191, 1903.

4. *Memoir on the Ruins of Babylon*, 1815 and *Second Memoir on Babylon*, 1818. His other work was *Narrative of a Residence in Koordistan* and on the site of *Ancient Nineveh*, with *Journal of a Voyage down the Tigris to Baghdad, and an account of a visit to Shiraz and Persepolis*, 1836. His collections are now in the British Museum.

5. The French Mission Archéologique was founded at almost the same time.

6. *My First Hundred Years*, 1963, p. 111.

7. Op. cit., p. 153.

8. *A Hundred and Fifty years of Archaeology*, p. 406.

9. Ibid, p. 92.

10. Such an attitude was not peculiar to British excavations. The American archaeologist, George Reisner, held very similar views. He went to Egypt in 1897 and worked there until he died in 1942, living at the Howard-Boston camp near the Pyramids. His recipe for success was that 'good pay, steady work, kind but firm treatment, must be the basis of all oriental faithfulness. Good work and faithfulness must be rewarded and the opposite punished. Mistakes in this matter are fatal.' In his obituary of Reisner (*Antiquity*, vol. XVII, no. 67, September 1963), J. W. Crowfoot wrote: 'He was innocent of the acquisitive foibles of an older generation of antiquaries and a Puritan of the Puritans in the matter of the purchase of small antiquities, knowing how much science has suffered from clandestine digging in Egypt and how easily an excavation camp may be turned into a den of thieves'.

11. Margaret Murray, op. cit., p. 117.

12. Later Keeper of the Ashmolean. There was considerable irony in the fact that he eventually came to hold the same post as Arthur Evans.

13. Joan Evans *Time and Chance*, 1943, p. 340.

14. Quoted in Joan Evans, *Time and Chance*, p. 341.

15. Ibid, p. 351.

16. Preface to the English edition of Emil Ludwig's *Schliemann of Troy: the Story of a Gold-Seeker*, 1931.

17. On this, see Lynn and Gray Poole, *One Passion, Two Loves: the Schliemanns of Troy*, 1962, p. 171.

18. *Spadework: Adventures in Archaeology*, 1953, p. 11.

19. *Adventures in Archaeology*, p. 17.

20. This was a prestigious organisation. It had been founded in 1898, under the patronage of Kaiser Wilhelm II and received considerable financial support from the State.

21. 1938 Pelican edition, pp. 51–2.

22. *Spadework*, p. 63.

23. *Mallowan's Memoirs*, 1977, p. 302.

CHAPTER 4

1. Preface to the volume for 1871.

2. His autobiography, *Said and Done*, 1955, is very useful in this respect.

3. *Antiquity*, vol. X, no. 40, December 1936, p. 386.

4. Vol. XI, no. 37, March 1938.

5. *Antiquaries Journal*, vol. 57, part I, 1977, pp. 7–8.

6. *Mallowan's Memoirs*, 1977, pp. 237–8.

7. Wheeler's first attempts at involving commercial interests had been ten years earlier at Caerleon, when he had scandalised the traditionalists by getting money from the *Daily Mail* – see *Archaeologia*, vol. MCMXXVIII, pp 111–12.

8. Eric C. Gee, a Birmingham undergraduate. Undated letter in the archives of the Dorset Archaeological Society.

9. Letter dated 8 October 1936, in the archives of the Dorset County Museum.

10. Letter to Col. Drew, 13 July 1936, in the archives of the Dorset County Museum.

11. Ronald W. Clark, *Sir Mortimer Wheeler*, 1960, pp. 65–6.

12. *Dorset County Chronicle*, 19 September 1935.

13. Sir Mortimer Wheeler, *Still Digging*, 1955, pp. 104–5.

14. *Still Digging*, 1955, p. 72. One young archaeologist who learned a great deal as a result of working with Wheeler was Dame Kathleen Kenyon, who from 1930, when she was 24, until 1935 was a leading member of the considerable staff employed at Verulamium. After a distinguished archaeological career, especially in the Near East, she became Principal of St Hugh's College, Oxford. She was, as *The Times'* obituary put it, 'a forceful character, greatly loved by all who worked with her'. Forcefulness was a helpful quality for anyone, male or female, who had to deal satisfactorily with Mortimer Wheeler. It did Dame Kathleen no harm either to have been the daughter of a greatly respected Director of the British Museum, Sir Frederic Kenyon.

15. 17th March, 1976.

16. 1957.

17. 1978.

18. *CBA Newsletter and Calendar*, July 1979.

CHAPTER 5

1. What follows is a summary of a long recorded discussion with Dr Radford in

June 1978. His eminence as an archaeologist, combined with his remarkable memory, unflagging energy and his wide circle of friends and delightful sense of humour, makes Dr Radford unequalled as a source of information about the personalities of British archaeology over a period of more than half a century.

2. *CBA Newsletter and Calendar*, April 1979.

3. *CBA Calendar and Newsletter*, April 1979. The 'Notes' were not written specially for this particular issue. They had been in circulation for some time previously.

4. *Local History in England*, 1959, pp. 3–4.

5. Reprinted in *The Listener*, 20 January 1972, p. 68.

6. *Antiquaries Journal*, vol. XLIX, part 1, 1969, p. 32.

7. This has been equally true at York, where the work during the early 1970s was on a very large scale and several hundred people took part in the excavation each year. For the financing and labout force at York, see P. V. Addyman, 'Excavations at York', *Antiquaries Journal*, vol. LIV, part 2, 1974, pp. 200–201.

8. *Antiquaries Journal*, vol. L, part 2, 1970.

9. Council for British Archaeology, *Report No. 21 for the year ended 30 June 1971*, p. 15.

10. Ibid, p. 16.

11. *Archaeology in Britain, 1972–73*, p. 96.

12. Ibid, p. 96.

13. *Archaeology in Britain, 1972–73*, p. 8.

14. *Archaeology in Britain, 1977*, p. 7.

15. *Archaeology in Britain, 1975–76*, p. 46.

16. Ibid, p. 46.

CHAPTER 6

1. *Industrial Archaeology Magazine*, a popular quarterly which began publication in the Summer of 1979, is entirely concerned with objects, with relics. It is for 'dedicated preservationists'.

2. Kenneth Hudson, *Industrial Archaeology: an Introduction*, 1963.

3. Vol. 1, no. 1, May 1964, p. 1.

4. Roy Lewis and Rosemary Stewart, in *The Boss: the Life and Times of the British Business Man*, p. 34.

5. p. 91.

6. Preface.

7. p. 153.

8. Vol. 3, no. 3, August 1966.

9. Vol. 5, no. 1, February 1968.

10. Vol. 11, no. 3.

11. On the early history of the Record, see Dr R. A. Buchanan (ed), *The Theory and Practice of Industrial Archaeology*, 1968, pp. 4–10.

12. Op. cit., p. 5.

13. Vol. 3, no. 3, August 1966, p. 239.

14. See *Industrial Archaeology*, vol. 4, no. 3, August 1967, p. 281.

15. *The Theory and Practice of Industrial Archaeology*, p. 6.

16. *The Theory and Practice of Industrial Archaeology*, p. 6.

17. 'Post-post-medieval archaeology', *Antiquity*, vol. XLVII, 1973, p. 215.

18. Op cit., p. 215. For variations on the same theme, see two articles in *Industrial Archaeology*, Iain Walker, 'Whither industrial archaeology', vol. 13, no. 3, Autumn 1978, and Peter Conlan, 'Will IA develop a clear role?', vol. 14, no. 1, Spring 1979.

19. In *Industrial Archaeology: a New Introduction*, 1976, pp. 21–24.

Bibliography

Most books and articles dealing with the history of archaeology have been concerned primarily with the development of the philosophy and techniques of the subject and only incidentally with its practitioners and its place within the contemporary climate of opinion. The best general guide for those whose main need is to establish a general framework of ideas is Glyn Daniel's invaluable *150 Years of Archaeology*, 1975, a revised edition of a book first published in 1950 as *A Hundred Years of Archaeology*. The bibliography of this book remains unequalled as a reference source for those whose main concern is with theories and achievements, rather than with people. Professor Daniel's book, like its bibliography, covers the growth of world archaeology as a whole. An excellent summary of the same trends is to be found in the introduction to Jacquetta Hawkes, *The World of the Past*, 1963. J. O. Brew, *One Hundred Years of Anthropology* necessarily has much to say about archaeology as well, with a very detailed bibliography, and Stanley Casson, *The Discovery of Man*, 1939, provides an excellent historical survey of the closely linked progress of both archaeology and anthropology.

Useful clues to the atmosphere in which archaeological work took place in the earlier years of the present century are to be found in J. Baikie, *The Glamour of Near East Excavations*, 1927; R. V. D. Magoffin and E. C. Davis, *The Romance of Archaeology*, 1923; D. Masters, *The Romance of Excavations*, 1923; and J. Baikie, *A Century of Excavation in the Land of the Pharaohs*, 1926.

More recent works which help to establish the social context of archaeology are A. T. White, *Lost Worlds: Adventures in Archaeology*, 1947; K. B. Shippen, *Men of Archaeology*, 1963; Joan Evans, *A History of The Society of Antiquaries of London*, 1956; J. Rodden, *A History of British Archaeology*, 1975; D. Hawkins, *Cranborne Chase*, 1980.

The biographies and autobiographies which I have found particularly valuable are: C. Breasted, *Pioneer to the Past: the Story of J. H. Breasted, Archaeologist*, 1948; Mrs A. G. Duff, *The Life and Work of Lord Avebury*, 1924; L. and G. Poole, *One Passion, Two Loves: the Schliemanns of Troy*, 1967; Katherine M. Lyell, *Life, Letters and Journals of Sir Charles Lyell*, 1881; Ronald Clark, *Sir Mortimer Wheeler*, 1960; Joan Evans, *Time and Chance*, 1943; O. G. S. Crawford, *Said and Done*, 1955; A. H. Layard, *Autobiography and Letters*, 1903; Sir Leonard Woolley, *Spadework*, 1953; Sir Mortimer Wheeler, *Still Digging*, 1955; Sir Flinders Petrie, *Seventy Years of Archeology*, 1931; Margaret Murray, *My First Hundred Years*, 1963.

Obituaries in newspapers and periodicals are probably the richest mine of information about archaeologists great and small, and I have relied extensively on them, not only for the personal details they enshrine, but also for the way in which they reflect contemporary attitudes to the people concerned and to their chosen field of activity. In this connection I have derived both pleasure and profit from tributes to be found in *The Antiquaries Journal, Antiquity, The Antiquary*, newspapers, especially *The Times*, and in the journals of the county archaeology societies.

I have been able to use unpublished material in the archives of Salisbury Museum, the Wiltshire Archaeological and Natural History Society, Somerset Archaeological and Natural History Society, the Dorsetshire Archaeological and Natural History Society and the Society of Antiquaries. The membership lists of these and other institutions are of great value in allowing one to gain an impression of kind as well as the number of people who have supported the archaeological cause at different periods, a line of research much helped by the photographic collections maintained by these bodies, which often supply both facts and perspective not easily obtained from words alone.

The contribution made by broadcasting to the popularisation of archaeology can be assessed by reading the appropriate sections of the annual *BBC Handbook* from 1950 onwards, from the files of *The Listener* and the *Radio Times*, from Paul Johnstone, *Buried Treasure*, 1957, and from *Chronicle: Essays from ten years of television archaeology*, edited by Ray Sutcliffe, 1978.

The year by year progress of archaeology in all its branches in this country is admirably documented by the annual reports of the Council for British Archaeology from 1944 onwards, supplemented in more recent years by its bi-monthly *Newsletter and Calendar*.

The social aspects of industrial archaeology have to be researched in rather a different way. Only two of the subject's notable practitioners, L. T. C. Rolt and Sir Arthur Elton, have so far died, so obituaries are not a great help here. The various periodicals devoted to industrial archaeology, in both its main and its sidestreams, are well worth combing for human and social information. *The Journal of Industrial Archaeology*, launched in 1964, became *Industrial Archaeology* in 1966 and then, ten years later, developed in a complicated fashion. The title, *Industrial Archaeology*, was appropriated by another firm of publishers, who claimed to be the rightful heirs to the kingdom, while the editor and advisory committee transferred themselves to the newly established *Industrial Archaeology Review*, published by the Oxford University Press and sponsored by the Association for Industrial Archaeology. In all these periodicals, the most useful information for the present purpose is to be found in the mini-biographies of contributors and in the regular *Notes and News* features.

Industrial Archaeology 1, but neither *Industrial Archaeology* nor *Industrial Archaeology Review* regularly included a list of relevant local societies. *Industrial Archaeologists' Guide*, 1971–73, in the section relating to societies and organisations, pp. 121–147, indicates those societies which at that time produced newsletters or journals and set out the fields in which each society was particularly interested.

Index